The

ULTIMATE

MOM

**Uplifting Stories, Endearing Photos,
and the Best Experts' Tips on the
Toughest Job You'll Ever Love**

Maria Bailey
Host of *Mom Talk Radio* and Founder of NewBaby.com

Health Communications, Inc.
HCI Books, the Life Issues Publisher
Deerfield Beach, Florida

www.hcibooks.com
www.ultimatehcibooks.com

We would like to acknowledge the writers and photographers who granted us permission to use their material. Copyright credits for interior photographs appear on each photograph and credits for literary work are listed alphabetically by authors' last names. Contact information as supplied by the photographers and writers can be found in the back matter of this book.

With Mom's Love. ©Judy L. Adourian. All rights reserved.

When You Least Expect It. ©Maria Bailey. All rights reserved.

Exa. ©B. J. Bateman. All rights reserved.

The Impromptu Birthday. ©Jane Koenen Bretl. All rights reserved.

(*Copyright credits continued on page 273*)

**Library of Congress Cataloging-in-Publication Data
is available through the Library of Congress.**

©2009 Maria Bailey

ISBN-13: 978-0-7573-0796-6
ISBN-10: 0-7573-0796-5

Publisher: Health Communications, Inc.
          3201 S.W. 15th Street
          Deerfield Beach, FL 33442-8190

Cover Design: Justin Rotkowitz
Cover Photo: © *Purestock*
Photo Editor: Justin Rotkowitz
Interior Design: Lawna Patterson Oldfield

*To the four wonderful people
who call me Mom:
Madison, Owen, Keenan, and Morgan.
I strive to be the "Ultimate Mom,"
touching your lives in ultimate ways.*

Is something "Ultimately" important to you?
Then we want to know about it. . . .

We hope you enjoyed *The Ultimate Mom*. We are planning many more books in the Ultimate series, each filled with entertaining stories, must-know facts, and captivating photos. We're always looking for talented writers to share slice-of-life true stories, creative photographers to capture images that a story can't tell, as well as top experts to offer their unique insights on a given topic.

For more information on submission guidelines, or to suggest a topic for an upcoming book, please visit the Ultimate website at **www.ultimatehcibooks.com**, or write to: Submission Guidelines, Ultimate Series, HCI Books, 3201 SW 15th St., Deerfield Beach, FL 33442.

For more information about other books by Health Communications, Inc., please visit **www.hcibooks.com**.

Contents

New Beginnings

The Wind Beneath Our Wings

Mentoring Moms

Memories of Mom

Must-Know Info

Introduction

or What It *Really* Means to Be the Ultimate Mom

Motherhood. There are few words in the English language that hold so much meaning and even fewer that are so undefined. As a noun, it's an identity that is customized by the women who possess it, and as a destination, it's a role entered into in many different ways. It's a life stage that even girls as young as two years old strive to obtain. We see it in the faces of ponytailed toddlers when they hold their baby dolls close to their breast and rock them gently, singing the lyrics to their favorite lullaby. As teenagers, hormonal mothers-to-be practice their skills for motherhood by babysitting. The desire to obtain the state of motherhood is so strong in some women that it triggers an internal clock that some tie to biology, but in reality it is the innate need to nurture and love unconditionally.

Entering the world of motherhood can come in many different ways. Four million women a year give birth to babies in the United States, while more than 250,000 adopt children from within the country or beyond our borders. Others marry into the role of motherhood, committing to nurture children from another marriage or foster little people who yearn for the warmth of a mother's love.

Sometimes a woman takes on the role of Mom without sharing biology or even the same home. There are plenty of aunts, friends, and caretakers who could just as fully be called Mom.

Once we enter into motherhood, the names we choose to identify our newly acquired state of mutual dependency are as numerous as the journey that takes us there: Mother, Mom, Madre, Mama, and Mommy. However, it's not only the name we respond to that joins us to our children, but the voice that projects it. Mothers come with a sixth sense that allows them to identify with the right "mom," even when it's hollered in the middle of a crowded mall. Regardless of the number of other moms in the same space, we seem to know that it's our child who's in need.

Motherhood is a remarkable experience, and just as no two mothers are exactly alike, just as no two moms enter into the state of motherhood in the same fashion, and just as no two mommies care for their children in the same way, the experience it brings to our lives is as varied. Ironically, however, in the variety that motherhood presents to the millions of women who have been bestowed with its joys, sorrows, disappointments, fatigue, and happiness, it would be difficult to find one mother who would give up her title of Mom. It's the one commonality of the word motherhood—the mutual feelings of love, dedication, and commitment that are shared by all moms.

I've been privileged during my adult life to be immersed in the world of mothers. On a personal level, God has blessed me with four beautiful children: Madison, Owen, Keenan, and Morgan. They did not enter my life in the manner that I believed they would when I dreamed of becoming a mother, but none of that matters now. I wouldn't change a thing about the way I became a mother or the children I have in my family. You can read my own story of motherhood in "New Beginnings." I hope it touches you the way it has touched eleven other wannabe moms that heard about my journey into motherhood and followed the path I took. They now celebrate first steps, birthdays, report cards, and all the things they once thought they would miss as childless women. I feel so fortunate that my own story of motherhood has helped others realize the dream of having a child in their lives.

Professionally, moms have become my business. I realized in the late 1990s when I was the mother of three children under twenty months old that companies and the media were not speaking to me as a consumer of goods and information. I watched ads that depicted mothers as diaper-slinging women who were unfit and adorned in oversized sweatpants, and when I got into the car, I listened to a medley of kid's tunes on Radio Disney or sports talk on the radio. There was nothing for me—a solution-starved mom who wanted to relish my womanhood as well as my motherhood. So I did what any sane, time-starved mother of three babies would do—I wrote a book and started a radio show.

My book, *Marketing to Moms: Getting Your Share of the Trillion Dollar Market*, was the first to quantify the annual spending of moms—something that even the U.S. government hadn't done. To the amazement of many, the $1.7 trillion mothers spent in 1999 was more than the gross national product of Spain, Portugal, and Australia combined. In fact, mothers are the largest consumer group in the United States, yet few companies at that time were paying attention to us. I am happy to report that after two more books on the mom market, *Trillion Dollar Moms: Marketing to a New Generation of Mothers* (Random House, 2005) and *Mom 3.0: Marketing with Today's Mothers by Leveraging New Media and Technology* (Wyatt-McKenzie, 2008), companies today take mothers very seriously. You can see this by the products they produce to make motherhood a little bit easier to the manner in which we are depicted on television and in advertising. Say what you will about moms such as Angelina Jolie, Hillary Clinton, Sarah Palin, or even Britney Spears, these women have helped bring attention to the job of motherhood.

I entered the world of radio with the launch of *Mom Talk Radio* in December 1999. It was the first nationally syndicated radio show for moms. Truthfully, I didn't know a thing about radio, but I did know that moms were searching for information and that they were in their cars more hours a day than anyone else. Today *Mom Talk Radio* (www.momtalkradio.com) has more than a half million listeners from South Florida to South Africa and is available on traditional radio as well as online and as a podcast via iTunes and other podcast outlets. The show offers interviews with experts, authors, and celebrity moms.

My passion for mothers has given birth to my marketing firm, BSM Media, which consults with companies such as Disney, Hewlett-Packard, Precious Moments, and Avon. We help brands develop product and marketing messaging that resonates with mothers and provides them with solutions to everyday challenges. Additionally, my love for connecting moms with information has led to the creation of BlueSuitMom.com (www.bluesuitmom.com), an award-winning website for working mothers and Newbaby.com (www.newbaby.com), a video portal for moms.

The journey of building a business based on motherhood has been one of many fulfilling milestones; however, the greatest gift has been the opportunity to meet thousands of mothers around the globe. From the Zulu moms in shack villages outside of Johannesburg, to the stroller striders along the shores of San Diego, to the hockey moms of Anchorage, to the pram pushers of Paris, I've met so many wonderful mothers along the way. A day doesn't go by that I am not thankful for the stories these women have shared with me, the e-mails filled with ideas on how to solve common problems, phone calls exchanging solutions, tweets stocked with opinions and emotion, and blog posts commenting on topics from sex to supersized grocery bills. The knowledge, insights, and advice that I've gathered from moms I've met along the way are invaluable. The appreciation for what can be gathered by mothers sharing their thoughts, emotions, and stories with other mothers is what brought me to the book you now hold in your hands. *The Ultimate Mom* is my way of bringing moms together through stories, some happy, some sad, but all told with the uniting voice of love, devotion, and dedication to their children. You will experience firsthand the diversity of the definition of motherhood while understanding the unifying bond between mothers. There's no better title on Earth than that of a mother and none as rewarding. Being an ultimate mom is the ultimate job.

Celebrating the Bond

The Real Mother

By Tracy Line

I t took me a long time to figure out I was a mother. Oh, I knew I had kids (how could I forget?), but me, a mother? I was more like a woman with children. You see, in my mind, a mother was so much more than I could ever be.

I'll never forget the day I discovered I was pregnant. Staring at that little white stick with the blue line, I wondered—how could it be? I didn't feel any different; I didn't look any different, but suddenly, I was different. I remember pondering, *What kind of mother will I be?* I thought I would soon know, but I was wrong.

Nine months later, I lay in my hospital bed, staring at our little pink bundle with awe (or perhaps it was fear). I knew nothing about this little person whom I held in my arms except that it was my job to raise her. I do remember the nurse telling my husband what a nice family we had. Family? We weren't a *family*. A family is two kids, a dog, and a mortgage, along with a mother who knew what she was doing. Others may have defined us as a family, but in my book we were just us, plus her.

We took our baby home and life went on. My husband and I did what all young parents do; we fumbled. We naively made our

way through colic and midnight feedings and spit-up. That first
year was full of ups and downs. I felt such joy and love for my girl,
yet I was also overwhelmed from the responsibilities of being a
working mother. My husband was there to help, but even so, I
felt completely alone in my passage to motherhood. The roles of
Helper and One-in-Charge were clearly established. *I* was the one
responsible for soothing her cries, rocking her to sleep, teaching
her how to share; he would help.

The problem was I didn't always know how to do these things.
Sometimes I couldn't get my girl to stop crying or settle down to
sleep, and she didn't always share. It seemed there was a discon-
nection. I often watched other mothers in action and wondered
how they did it. How come they had everything they needed in
the diaper bag while I left mine at home? How did they get their
toddler to stop running through the mall, while mine just laughed
and ran faster? The first years of motherhood left me feeling
inadequate. A real mother would know what to do; for me, it was
hit or miss all the way.

One thing I did have down was the guilt. I'd heard other mothers say they couldn't bear to leave their children. Me? I longed to
sleep through the night or eat a meal without interruption. No
one else seemed to want that. Real mothers, I thought, aren't so
selfish. They care for their babies with love and patience. I did,
too, but I didn't feel like it. Not that I didn't love my girl; I did. I
just found that being a mother could be hard; it requires giving up
what you want to do what is best for your child. Was I the only
one who noticed that?

So what was a "real" mother in my book? Everything I wasn't.

Real mothers were calm and confident, much more sure of themselves than I was. They knew how to handle the unfathomable situations children put you in. Real mothers had pot roast in the oven and a house that smelled of clean laundry. They were prepared; toys and snacks in the diaper bag, tissues and wipes in the van. I had a ten-year-old sedan and a diaper bag with stale crackers and an empty tube of Desitin. Real mothers, not wannabes like me, had the knowledge, confidence, and supplies. I wasn't in their league.

Maybe, I thought, I could learn to be one of those mothers. I turned to the experts and read book after book after book. But instead of answers, all I got was confusion. Oh, there was plenty of advice out there; the trouble was that it was all paradoxical. If I wanted to discipline my child, I should be loving and firm, but not harsh. I should be consistent yet flexible, but maintain a solid routine. No one had advice for how to fit in a shower, convince a thirteen-month-old to get dressed, or keep her away from the dog food bowl. The books weren't helping.

Next I turned to those around me. I'd observe my friends who were mothers, hoping to pick up a tidbit or two. Yet no two were alike. Each touted an individual philosophy on everything from feedings, to naps, to discipline. One friend never raised her voice or worried about behavior; no eighteen-year-old bites, she pointed out. I had to agree that most adults were potty trained and did not go around yelling "No! By self!" Yet, as I sat one day and watched her children squirt ketchup all over each other, I decided I couldn't just wait for eighteen.

Older ladies quickly became my friends. I'd sit on a mall bench to tie a shoe or give my child a snack and find myself chatting with a senior. But I got little advice. Mostly I learned that these years would fly by. One day I would wake up and there would be no toys on the floor or Cheerios on the table, and the house would be too quiet. I hated to hear it; not because I dreaded that time, but because it sounded really peaceful.

But those ladies were right; the years did fly by. Baby number two arrived and life got busier. Birthday parties, trips to the zoo; if I never had to go to another fast-food playland, I couldn't be happier. We were knee-deep in toys, school papers, soccer, and Nickelodeon. Sometimes things would go smoothly, but this never lasted. Always, something like a round of the flu, a "nice" family outing, or a completely unforeseen tantrum would shake things up and I'd blow under the pressure. Or, I'd show up at church with shoes that didn't match and toothpaste on my skirt only to run into one of those "together" mothers smiling at me. All the old feelings would resurface; I was a wannabe, never the real mother I *should* be.

Then came Abigail. She was our third, our change-of-heart child. This girl made me realize what a real mother I am. Did having three make me more motherly, more together? Heck, no. If anything, I am busier and more behind than ever; but I'm happy. Having a third child allowed me to give up striving for the ideal and become content with well-adjusted and crazy. Somehow in the chaos I learned to look at life differently. My vision of motherhood shifted. I discovered that being a real mother isn't about having it all together, looking perfect, or having a serene life. It is about being there for your children and trying to do what is best for your family even when you aren't sure what that is.

I spent the first years of motherhood in search of the perfect mother and trying to be her. Now I know that I'll never be perfect, but I will always be a mother. I've been there day in and day out for my children. I've brushed away tears, made dinosaur birthday cakes, and stayed up late to help build a log cabin for Pioneer Day. I've done a few things right and many things wrong. But through it all, I have loved my children and they know it. Does anything else really matter?

Real mothers aren't perfect. They yell, cry, and sometimes fantasize about escaping. They don't always show up on time, and occasionally they have toothpaste on their skirt. Yet real mothers do what they must for their children. They go without sleep to hold a sick child, spend too much money on school fund-raisers, and love their children even when they are unlovable. They do it because that's what love is all about and someone once did it for them.

And those mothers I was in awe over long ago? They're not perfect either. Their perfection was only a facade born out of my own insecurities. All mothers struggle from time to time, whether they admit it or not.

Mothers come in all shapes and sizes. No two are quite the same. Yet we are similar in that we all experience a multitude of emotions when it comes to our children. We are all real, and whether we admit it or not, we relish a good night's sleep and a meal without interruption. Me? I'm still carrying that diaper bag, complete with the empty tube of Desitin and stale crackers. But now, I carry it proudly.

It's Chestnuts

By Andrea Marcusa

I haven't noticed chestnuts for years. But there they are high up and pale green, swinging from the tree branches and dropping with a thunk to the sidewalk. Most land intact, their thorny exteriors protecting the treasure that lies within. "It's chestnuts," I say to Mike and Daniel. Mike hops off the back of the stroller while his brother twists around to watch him. He stoops over and examines the spiked sphere then looks back at me.

"Go ahead, stomp on it," I say. Mike touches it with the toe of his sneaker. "No, harder." He presses his heel down and the green orb exposes the white flesh inside. He looks up puzzled. "Like this," I say. My swift step produces a shiny, reddish-brown prize. "That's a chestnut."

Mike bends over and seizes it. "Chestnut! It's so shiny!" Daniel strains under his stroller harness. I unbuckle him and the two run up and down the Central Park walkway finding chestnuts to stomp on. "Big one!" says Daniel, as he holds a chestnut in his small fingers. "This one has two!" Mike says, as he stuffs them into bulging pockets. I rest my hands on the stroller beneath the chestnut trees arching high overhead and feel something lift up inside of me. It's a thrill that I had stopped having a long time ago, an old lost treasure returned.

Before Mike and Daniel were born, on the rare day I stayed home from work, I would hear the sounds of children's laughter from the school nearby as kids ran around on the school's rooftop for recess. Their high-pitched voices blared above the sound of cars and the din of air conditioning below. I always found them pleasantly dissonant to the life I so diligently pursued.

One day I stayed home from work sick with a cold. At three o'clock, I went to the corner to buy orange juice. There all around me were kids coming home from school. Some wore sports uniforms, others carried knapsacks, while younger children grasped their mother's or nanny's hands as they traveled in a parallel world that I knew little about. So strange, I had thought. Not me, I had said as I tried to imagine myself with a child. I was busy taking hold of the adult world, solving weighty problems at meetings that swallowed up dinnertime or on 6:00 AM flights out of LaGuardia fanning to points south, north, or west. I once colored in a map of the United States to see how many states I'd traveled to, a testament to my newfound authority and importance.

As life so inevitably teaches us, I eventually moved beyond "Not me" and gave birth to two sons, unaware of what this life experience would offer. I had heard all the quaint sayings about blessings and little miracles, but those words always had the far-away feel of my grandparents' stories about the days before television. Sure, I knew that having children would teach me new skills, mostly the custodial ones needed to feed and care for a child, since I had entered adulthood with none. I counted on children linking me to the future and hoped my genes would have some small influence on generations to come.

I didn't really know how much motherhood would connect me to my past. With Mike and Daniel today on the sidewalk, I am both a delighted mother, relishing my sons' excited shrieks, and the young child I'd all but forgotten about.

Today I return to the time I spent in my neighbor's yard, hunting for chestnuts alone because my sister had declared herself too big for them. I feel the cool, dry breeze blowing the skirt of my new cotton paisley dress that my mother had sewn from a Butterick pattern. I am the nine-year-old who woke up every day excited about events that were then brand-new.

This same enthusiasm rushes back today as I say, "I used to love to do this!" I find my own bright green sphere and roll it under the ball of my foot. This seemingly inconsequential activity carries the weighty significance that could only be conjured in a child's mind, those soaring emotions felt pressing a buzzer on Halloween night or the ones that crash with a fall to the pavement and a skinned knee.

I kept the chestnuts for months in a shopping bag in my room. Soon, fall faded into winter and I would dump the chestnuts out of the bag under a tree for the squirrels to feast on during the freezing months. With spring's arrival I'd wear a lighter jacket and feel in a pocket the one prize chestnut I had saved because of its glossy coat or perfect shape. Upon examination, I'd see how a few short months had aged it. My perfect specimen had withered and lay pinched and wrinkled in my hand, its coppery color faded to dull brown.

Today with Mike and Daniel, I am seeing chestnuts for the first time without knowing what comes next. I hold one in my palm while the boys place the ones that won't fit into their pockets onto the stroller seat. We are consumed with the hunt. I marvel at the energy that propels their tiny legs up and down the walkway. I press a chestnut against my face and feel its cool slippery coat on my skin. The chestnut is larger than most with a deep reddish-brown coat. It's impossible to place this beautiful chestnut with the others. I hold on to it while I gather the boys on our walk toward home, then slip it into my pocket, secretly hoping that this time, the chestnut and today will last forever.

La Famiglia Pombo

By Connie K. Pombo

"**H**oney, it's time!" I gasped.

"Time for what?" my husband responded.

I pointed to the marble floor and the puddle of "water" that I was wading in. Mark—my hubby of five years—glanced down at the vast "ocean" that lay between my feet and asked, "Did you do that on purpose?"

There's something about pregnancy that will always remain foreign to men. They just can't relate to the cravings, mood swings, ever-expanding tummy, strange sensations, and the emotions that accompany being a first-time mom—especially when that first time happens to be in a foreign country like Italy!

We had just moved to the land of "la dolce vita" to teach English as a second language when we were surprised—shocked really—to find out that I was three months *incinta* (pregnant)!

"Call the doctor and the clinic," I responded calmly.

Mark rushed to the phone and punched in the numbers for La Villa Sant'Andrea Clinica where I would deliver our firstborn. And then he called the doctor, who I had only seen twice during my entire pregnancy—once to confirm I was actually pregnant and the second time just two days before my water broke.

While Mark scurried around our tiny apartment to gather up items to load in the car, I took a leisurely shower. I was four days past my due date and distracted myself by trying to look present-able for my new arrival. After my shower, I put on an extra coat of "Pretty in Pink" nail polish—hoping that would somehow guarantee me a baby girl.

As I waddled into the bedroom to grab my bag of "labor equip-ment," I bent over one last time—holding my tummy—and thought, *This is it; there's no turning back now!*

Mark helped me down three flights of stairs and into our Fiat 127, along with a pillow to sit on for the bumpy ride along crooked back roads to the clinic.

"Are you okay?" Mark asked, as he adjusted my pillow.

"Oh, I'm just *fine!* You know this is all your fault, don't you?" I snapped back. Mark ignored my outburst and continued to drive faster.

While I hissed, panted, and breathed slowly, Mark threaded in and out of traffic trying to race through every red light. I handed him my white pillowcase to hang out the window—the Italian signal that there was an emergency.

When we arrived at the clinic, Mark rang the intercom.

"*Pronto, chi parla?* (Who's there?)" the nurse asked.

"*La famiglia Pombo sta qui* (The Pombo family is here)," my hus-band responded.

That had a "foreign" sound to it. *A family?* I never quite thought of us that way until now. Soon there would be three of us, and our status as a couple would change forever.

The nurse greeted us warmly and helped me into the exam room where the intern waited impatiently. He examined me and announced, "Just one centimeter!"

The doctor explained—partly in English and mostly in Italian—that I would deliver sometime the following evening.

Mark patted me gently on the back as I leaned hard into his chest. "I don't think I can do this," I whimpered.

"Oh sure you can . . . just nine more centimeters to go," he added cheerfully.

That's when I realized labor was really *foreign* to men.

The nurse helped me off the exam table as I waddled to the chair to put on my labor gown. In Italy, you bring your own things to the hospital, so I packed a pink one and a blue one.

I chose pink!

"*Avanti, Signora Pombo* (Come along, Mrs. Pombo)," said the nurse.

There weren't any labor rooms available, so I was placed in the delivery room. In my labor bag, I had packed some earplugs just in case. I heard rumors that labor could get noisy. Strangely enough, no matter what country you are in, the birth process is the same—there is always a lot of screaming.

Although we had attended two classes of Lamaze training, *this* was not what I had signed up for: no labor room, no privacy, and two Italian women in labor shouting, "*Aiutami!* (Help me!)"

Mark reminded me of the importance of rest because I had a long twenty-four hours ahead of me. He rolled me over onto my left side, slumped down in the chair beside me, and gently rubbed my back.

At 3:01 AM—just three hours after we arrived at the clinic—I awoke with a strange, inexplicable urge to push, like a hiccup that had gone bad. Mark was snoring peacefully until I shook him awake.

"Mark, it's time. Get the doctor now . . . I'm going to have a baby!" I screamed.

"I know, honey, that's why we're here. Now go back to sleep," he whispered.

"*No*, I mean *now!*" I shouted.

There was no amount of heeing and hawing that was going to stop this baby; no amount of panting or chanting that was going to reverse this process.

The nurse came in to examine me and said, "*Buono!* (Good!)"

Mark translated it for me, "You can push now, sweetheart!"

There was no holding back—from Italy with love—I was going to be a *mamma*, and that's all there was to it. *But it wasn't supposed to be this way; I wanted to have a labor—not a delivery.* I didn't even get to use my well-practiced breathing techniques, and *now* I was *pushing*. The nurses wheeled me into an adjacent delivery room, just in time for the doctor to deliver an eight-pound four-ounce *bambino*.

"*Tanti auguri, Mamma!* (Congratulations, Mom!)," the nurses chimed in unison.

I watched as my red-faced bundle of joy received his first bath while tears made a path down my cheeks. It wasn't exactly what I had in mind for a first birth experience, but somehow it was just *perfect*.

In Italy, having a boy is considered good luck—especially for your first birth. And I had heard stories that some Italian husbands promised their wives diamond rings if they could bear them a son.

"Honey, where's my diamond ring?" I whispered.

Mark laid Geremia in my arms and said, "Here's your diamond, Mrs. Pombo!" It was a moment of wonder, ecstasy, and delight. I was finally a mom.

Geremia Cristofero Pombo was born on June 30, 1981, in the same town in which my husband's grandparents were born. I bore a son on foreign ground and lived to tell about it!

There's nothing quite like being a first-time mom, whether it's in a foreign country or in your own backyard. What seems *foreign* at first becomes natural with time. It all begins with the word *Mamma.*

♡

Mom, You're Not Going to *Write* About This, Are You?

By Mimi Greenwood Knight

My daughter recently went to her first dance. Her anxiety over the evening wasn't that of a normal fifteen-year-old girl: *What should I wear? Will my parents embarrass me when he picks me up? Will he try to kiss me good night?* No, the first words out of Haley's mouth after the young man called were, "Mom, you're not going to *write* about this, are you?" Such is your plight when you're the offspring of a writer, especially when your mom's favorite topic to write about is—YOU.

While some kids might cringe to overhear their mother tell a neighbor about their latest social faux pas, my kids have to worry that their exploits will be broadcast to the world at large. To hear them tell it, every embarrassing thing that they've ever done or said has been publicized in magazines, anthologies, and on the Internet.

Okay, I'll admit it's partially true. Over the years, Molly wet her pants, Hewson mooned a church congregation, Haley picked her nose through her dance recital, and Jonah stood behind a fat man and hollered, "Don't worry, Mom. I'm not going to ask you why he's so fat until we get in the car," all later chronicled for a national audience.

I try to remind them that the money I earn "narcing" on them allows me to stay at home and still be able to have some of the extras in life. They are not assuaged. The long lead time on most stories only makes matters worse. I might sell an essay today only to have it sit in a magazine's inventory for years before it actually makes it onto the page. That means the essay I wrote about Hewson playing an entire baseball game with his "cup" upside down when he was eight didn't make it into print until he was an eleven-year-old superjock.

The story about Molly's preschool streaking phase was published when she was seven. Haley's public inquiry about her grandmother's enema bag hit the magazine racks when she was in middle school (like middle school isn't excruciating enough), while Jonah's cat versus duct tape escapade is sitting in an inventory right now like a ticking time bomb just waiting to devastate him one day.

In my own defense though, sometimes the little boogers are just begging to be tattled on. Like the time we had to grease Hewson's head to get the training potty seat off. I'm going to keep that to *myself*? Or like the time Jonah swiped the surgical gloves in the pediatrician's exam room and then stashed them in his underpants so she wouldn't know he'd taken them, not realizing that she was going to *check the goods* during the exam and those rubber gloves would pop out of his little drawers like a jack-in-the-box. Now how do you *not* write about that?

How about the time when Molly mused out of the blue at age three, "Maybe the dish ran away with the spoon because they were under where the cow was going to land," or when Jonah offered matter-of-factly to our neighbor, "Well, hey, Miss Karen. You're getting old. Huh?" or any one of their self-induced haircuts, spatial experiments involving the neighbors' cat, or creative outdoor potty adventures?

How much self-control would it have taken to not write about this conversation I overheard when passing my boys' room one day?

Little brother (hollering): "Mom, I need some panties."

Big brother: "Man, you wear panties? Girls wear panties."

Little brother: "Well, what do you wear?"

Big brother: "Dude, I wear undies."

The other day, I was driving down the road with my four-year-old when he blurted out something absolutely hysterical. I laughed until I cried. When I finally caught my breath, he said, "Well, Mom?"

"Well, what?"

"Aren't you going to write that down?"

Am I that bad? You hear about the preacher's kids or children of politicians who feel like they're living in a fishbowl with their every move being scrutinized. I wonder how they'd feel if their foibles were exaggerated and embellished for optimum laugh potential as well.

Still, I tell my kids it could be worse. Farah Fawcett's son had to live with a mom who posed nude for *Playboy* at age fifty. The worst I ever did was write a story about them eating poop. Besides, as Anne LaMott so aptly puts it, "If they didn't want you to write about them, maybe they should have behaved themselves in the first place."

Reflections: You're a Mom . . . Always

By Marilyn Nutter

"**W**hat's new in your life?" my friend Susan asked as we met in the checkout line at the supermarket. "Well," I answered with a huge smile, "I'm going to be a grandmother!" Her response was a direct quote from two other friends who had heard my latest news: "Oh. How wonderful! You're about to embark on the most fantastic time of your life."

Yes, it was really quite strange. Every time my husband and I made our announcement, our friends who were grandparents gave the same response. My husband and I agreed that on August 25, our friends were right—this grandparent adventure got off to a fantastic start. Being the analytical person that I am, I tried to analyze it—what was it that made it so special? For one thing, I didn't have any physical pain! I could sit comfortably in a hard rocking chair an hour after our granddaughter was born and have no discomfort as I held her close and rocked away. No interruptions from a nurse to check on me. No soreness. Just pure joy! Three days later, my milk didn't come in, so I felt great! I didn't have any illusions about weight. Just because I could see my feet didn't mean that I thought I had lost thirty pounds! As a grandparent, nothing was new—I had already been through navel care, bottles, and nursing. I knew that I wouldn't drown the baby during her first bath. My list grew. I could actually enjoy uninterrupted sleep, unless I offered to get up in the middle of the night when I stayed at my daughter's house.

There were many things that made my first few days of grandparenting *grand*. But, at the same time, I was still a mom. The reality that my child had a beautiful baby moved me to tears, just as the first time I laid eyes on my daughter as a newborn. As I reflected on my first grandmother experience, I realized that there were many similarities between being a mom to my young children and being a mom to my adult daughter.

I had the privilege of being in the delivery room. I watched my daughter Heather in pain, and I watched her deliver her baby. As the labor became more intense, I heard myself say, "Good job . . . you're doing great . . . just a little more," and finally, "you did it!" I was a cheerleader in the delivery room just as I was when Heather was growing up. I remembered listening to her flawless performance at a piano recital and then watching months later as she froze and forgot what had been a perfectly memorized piece. I recalled working through best friend issues and boyfriend breakups. I remembered listening as she gave a speech, and as she showed me her exam results. I encouraged her in the delivery room just as I had encouraged her when she was a child and a teen.

Since my daughter and her husband lived out of state, I stayed in their home after the baby was born. I did the grocery shopping, housekeeping, laundry, and cooking. I met the physical needs of the home, and my acts of service were appreciated. My daughter and son-in-law thanked me for my ministry, but I thought, "What ministry?" You don't have to go halfway around the world to have a ministry; family is also our ministry, whether thanks is expressed or not.

I listened and picked up the baby when she cried. I offered comfort to her when she needed it. My daughter was exhausted and sometimes a little unsure of herself as a new mom. I remembered her insecurities as a young girl on the first day of school, when auditioning for a play, and when taking a test in a difficult subject. Availability and comfort were as necessary now as they were then.

Sometimes children cry without tears. I learned to listen to what my girls were saying between the lines. Were they refusing to wear a particular outfit because another child made fun of them? Did they decline an invitation to a friend's birthday party because they were afraid? Did they have fears about using a piece of gymnastics equipment? My daughter often asked me, "Mom, what do you think about . . . ? Though the issues were different, I think she was looking for validation of her thoughts and opinions just as when she was twelve.

Friday was my departure date and we talked on the previous Wednesday about leaving. "I think I've stayed a little too long." "Oh no!" she quickly answered. "I hope I haven't given you that impression. I'm not ready for you to leave." No, she hadn't given me that impression at all, but I knew that she needed to be on her own, whether she thought she was ready or not. She, her husband, and new daughter needed to be a family without me. I remembered dropping off my daughters at preschool or gymnastics, leaving them with a sitter for the first time, and saying good-bye at the college dorm. I knew that they would be fine, but secretly I wanted to peek and make sure. In those days I left and did what I needed to do, just as I left my daughter and her family now. I knew that Heather would be fine.

Sometimes as young moms we have to make hard choices for our children: What do they really need? What is best for them? Are they doing too many things and they're overtired—are there too many playdates? Have we signed up for too many activities? Do they need more rest than other children? Is their personality suited to activity or do they need more solitude? Do I need to say "no" when they want me to say "yes"?

Though our involvement and responses are at different levels as our children grow, we will always be a mom. My grandmother days have reminded me once again about being my child's best cheerleader and the need to listen to each child's individual needs and offer encouragement and comfort. Just wait until you become a grandmother—you get to do it all over again. And you know what? It's really quite *grand*.

♡

The Tiger Jigsaw Puzzle

By Joyce Stark

I remember that sunny June afternoon when Mom and I went up into her attic and I stared around me wide-eyed. It was like one enormous antique shop, and she was grinning at me as if she was proud of it all!

Mom is a hoarder, while I am a thrower-outer the minute it serves no useful purpose. I had lost count of the times she had promised to clear it out, but it was an argument I never seemed to win.

We looked at old kitchen chairs, old picture frames, my cradle, and even a set of knitting needles with a half-finished baby suit on it! There were lamps, tables, and folded drapes, and I realized when she had moved here about twenty years ago, she had brought most of her old home with her!

"You have to clear it out, Mom; none of this will ever be used!" I pointed out to her.

She shook her head, "You would be surprised what I have come up here for and am now using, bit by bit. I have no need to go out and spend a lot of money on something new because I have what I need up here!"

"What are all these little china dishes and plates?" I asked her. "You don't even like anything that is floral-patterned."

"Your cousin gave them to me when I broke my leg and couldn't get about. She always brought me a little something when she came to visit and to help me. I have a few downstairs; I use them for holding clips or screws. One by one, I will find a use for them," she explained.

"But Mom, why not just give them away in a yard sale or something?" I asked.

Mom sighed and her soft blue eyes stayed steadily on my face. "Because, they were given with love and I will not give them away carelessly and treat that love so shabbily!"

For the first time since I was a little girl, I heard a note of anger in my mom's gentle voice. I lowered my gaze and nodded, accepting her chastisement. I turned back to the stack of objects on my left and said, "Well, how about this old chair?"

"Your granddad used to sit in that old chair and carve little animals for me out of wood. I loved him so much, and he worked long, hard hours, but he would sit and take the time to make me little toys! I cannot part with that; it brings his smiling face to me every time I look at it."

So we went on, Mom and I, and for every object I mentioned, Mom had a story or a fond memory that made it impossible to get rid of it. As we went through things, I was finding out nice things about friends, relatives, and neighbors that I had never known before. All of these items were bonds that Mom had made with people, and I went from being irritated at her to wanting to hug her for being such a lovely lady.

Mom attracted warm and giving people because she was that way herself. My attic was empty, regularly tidied by me. I suddenly realized that I would go up there one day when I was Mom's age and I would have no memories at all. Not just that, but the links to people I loved and who loved me would not exist. I would just be a solitary figure in an immaculately clean attic!

"I have no logical reason for keeping your baby suit on these old knitting needles," Mom confessed, bringing me back to the present day. "It was just that your dad and I had tried for a baby for so long, and when you came along we were so happy!"

It was too much, I just suddenly grabbed hold of her and started to cry as I hugged her and said brokenly, to her amazement, "Mom, I love you so much!"

We went downstairs and had a cup of coffee, and I studied Mom. Had she sensed that recently I was a bit down? I realized that going up into the attic had been her idea, and she usually worked pretty hard to keep me out of there!

"Do you remember when you were about ten years old, you had a beautiful jigsaw puzzle of a tiger in the jungle?" she asked me.

I nodded, "Yes, but what I remember most was that there was one piece missing!"

"Well, I kept it anyhow, so here, you can have it back as a present from me, to start your attic collection!" she said handing it to me.

I sighed, "How come you actually had this down here, ready to give to me, and not up in the attic?"

She shrugged, "I am your mom. I love you and I know you. That is the first time you have cried in my arms for years!"

I suddenly grinned at her, "You knew, didn't you, that I've been down recently?"

"You make too much of perfection," she said. "None of the things up there are perfect—old chairs, half-finished knitting, chipped plates—but it doesn't matter, because they are perfect memories of people I met along the way."

"I know, Mom, the jigsaw isn't perfect, but it is still a lovely picture, right?" I asked her.

"Oh dear!" Mom exclaimed. "You will need to come here much more often. It has nothing to do with it being a lovely picture. It's to go up in your attic to remind you that you got it from your uncle Eric. He brought it back from India—all that way he brought it back, just because you loved tigers!"

As I finally left to walk to my car, the tiger jigsaw under my arm and Uncle Eric's telephone number in my purse, I laughed aloud. Mom had won again—thank goodness!

♡

Pit Stops
and Pitfalls

By Rachel Wallace-Oberle

Sometimes when I'm with a group of moms and we're swapping stories and chuckling at some of our finer moments, I find myself contributing an unforgettable example of my finesse in the parenting department. Nothing strengthens the mystical, mutual bond of motherhood quite as much as the confession of a thoroughly absurd predicament.

A few years ago my husband, Jay, our children, and I were traveling on the 401. Barrett and Thomas were about nine and six years old, and we were going to visit friends on the other side of Toronto in the village of Ajax. Thomas is notorious for his pit stops; it doesn't matter how many times he uses the bathroom before we leave the house, invariably the plaintive call goes up mere miles down the road.

In anticipation of these emergencies, I usually make sure an empty paper cup or something similar is on hand just in case we're in the middle of nowhere, but on this particular trip there was, alas, no paper cup to be found.

"Thomas, you'll have to wait until we get there," I explained.

"I can't," he said, looking around the car desperately.

"You'll have to," I said.

"But I can't," he wailed.

I wasn't sure what to do. There was no rest area in sight, and pulling over in the middle of rush hour on the 401 was out of the question. Then I spied an empty plastic grocery bag in the back, and suddenly my finely honed mothering instincts took over.

"Here, Thomas," I said, rolling down the edges of the bag to make a potty, "we'll use this."

Thomas looked at me as though I was mad. "A grocery bag?" he squeaked in disbelief.

"It's that or wait," I said. Jay was watching me incredulously in the rearview mirror. Barrett was practically doubled over with laughter in the front seat.

Thomas began to undo his little jeans, looking dubiously out the windows. Cars whizzed by oblivious to the drama unfolding in the blue Chevy minivan. Thomas began to utilize the grocery bag.

Everything seemed fine until I felt something soaking through my shoe. I looked down. A bright stream was spraying out of the bottom of the bag as fast as Thomas was filling it up.

"Thomas!" I screeched. "There's a hole in the bag!"

I will never forget the look on his face. He was utterly dumbfounded; it was as if the whole ludicrous situation suddenly became too much for his mind to comprehend.

"Hurry up!" I bellowed.

What exactly does one do with a leaking grocery bag of number one on the 401 during rush hour? It's a dilemma of mammoth proportions, but at that dire moment I made an executive decision. Once again, my superior mothering skills sprang into action;

I rolled down the window and heaved the whole shebang out-side. The wind snatched it and smacked it right back against the window I had just barely finished rolling up. Rivulets streamed down the glass and whipped around the back to run across the rear window.

As if that wasn't startling enough, a fierce gust then peeled away the still-dripping bag and hurled it across the highway, where it bounced crazily off the windshields of several stunned drivers. Then it soared off into the distance, a curious flapping creature against the sky.

At this point we were laughing so hysterically that Jay was hav-ing trouble driving.

"Look at it go!" Thomas shouted, pointing and howling with glee.

What is it about being a mother that simultaneously thrills, amazes, stirs, and humbles? I've had my stall door in a public washroom exuberantly flung open by Thomas; dignity definitely does a disappearing act when you're caught clutching a wad of toilet tissue with a pair of panty hose slithering around your ankles beside a spirited toddler. I have reached into my purse as a Sunday morning service is ending, desperate for a piece of gum to freshen my breath, only to find a bunch of empty wrappers and my children chewing happily in the pew beside me. I've had an entire grocery cart filled to the top overturn in the store while negotiating a corner with a child hanging on the side.

And like countless other mothers, I have plunked pungent bouquets of dandelions into Tupperware cups with tears in my eyes, taped pictures of grinning, toothless stick figures with four strands of hair and clubfeet entitled "My Mother" on the fridge, and worn necklaces made with string, Play-Doh, and love.

While I was growing up, convinced that my mother was doing most things wrong and certain that I would never repeat her grave errors, I planned to be a paragon of exemplary parenting, a font of wisdom, an adaptable, unflappable mother. My children would be perfectly behaved, quick to listen, clean and neat, but most of all, refined and well mannered. I remember a mortifying incident years ago when Barrett and Thomas had a sleepover at my best friend's and she informed me while I was picking them up that she had caught them spitting at people over the balcony of her fourth-floor apartment.

"They did not," I protested, gathering up their pajamas and pillows.

"They did, too," Cathy said.

"They wouldn't do that," I declared.

"They would, too," she said.

"I have never, ever seen them do such a thing!"

From the balcony we heard the unmistakable sounds of spitting. Cathy grinned at me.

"Told you so," she said cheerfully.

If anything, being a mother has taught me that pride has no place, plans are made to be broken, rules change constantly, dreams don't always come true, and zippers in snowsuits seldom last longer than six weeks. It's a profession of bewildering yet exhilarating proportions; qualifications are unnecessary, recognition is rare, and quitting time is nonexistent. The demands are colossal, but they are dwarfed by the rewards. Every day is an adventure. Every moment is precious. Every child is unique.

When my children are grown and become parents, I anticipate they'll make the same miraculous discovery I did: Mom's mistakes weren't as dreadful as imagined. I hope my children will be able to say of me that like the woman of virtue described in Proverbs 31, I open my mouth in wisdom and on my tongue is the law of kindness. I hope they will rise up and call me blessed and know that I fear the Lord. I hope they can say strength and honor are my clothing and that in our home hurts and adversity are soothed with the ointment of laughter, love, and grace.

If I can send my sons out into this world as men of honor and distinction, as men of God, then I will have done well. It's a responsibility and privilege beyond mothering or fathering; it's the living out and the passing on of all that is admirable, true, lovely, and good of the human spirit.

While at times I meet the challenges beautifully, often I fail. The road ahead will always be potholed with pit stops and pit-falls, but I believe that it's the way it's traveled and the tracks we leave that count.

Merriment
and Mishaps

The Impromptu Birthday

By Jane Koenen Bretl

W hen you have your precious new baby, his cute little diapers full of cute little poo-poo do not seem so bad. Diaper changing is just something you do as a mother, most days (and nights) with patience and gratitude that you have a healthy baby. Eventually though, even the most devoted parents hold fast to a fervent hope that someday their offspring will actually be toilet trained. What freedom—no more diapers!! But sometimes the process does not go as planned. . . .

We started talking to our son about using the bathroom when he was two. No pressure, mind you; we just read the requisite books on the topic, since, as we all know, *everybody poops*. We had the children of friends show how—look!—they can go potty all by themselves. We explained that it was no big deal; it was just what big boys do.

Nick was very precocious, intelligent, logical even, so by age three I already enjoyed having actual conversations with him. He was very tall for his age, which made him seem older. Once he could discuss mathematical concepts with me while I changed his diaper, I knew we needed to put this potty-training thing on the fast track. I knew he understood the concept and would do it when he was ready.

So, when he was three and a half, we had reached this critical roadblock on the road to potty training: Nick had convinced himself that since his best friend was four when he started using the toilet, he also *could not do it until he was four*. Period. He had absolutely, resolutely, completely convinced himself this was true. Nothing we said could change his mind. I tried all the advice in the parenting books, asked friends for help, tried different tactics for months, and still he was stuck at this hurdle. I feared making too big of a deal out of it (the word "anal-retentive" came to mind). There was no medical problem; it was all mental. He had convinced himself that he could not do it, and therefore he truly could *not* do it. He wanted to; he cried that he *couldn't*. He started to feel bad about himself, and that was the last thing that I wanted. This was a matter of mind over matter—and I knew he could do it. I believed in him.

What to do? The kid did not come with an instruction manual. So, one desperate morning in February, I woke up with an idea that quickly formed into a plan: if he believed he needed to be four, well then, we would just make him be four. That day. February 16. His "real" birthday was in July. Luckily, although he was intelligent for his age, he did not yet have a firm grasp of the calendar. I went into his room that morning and delivered the good news.

"Good morning, big boy! Happy Birthday!!!"

"Today is my *birthday*??? Yeah!!" Birthdays are all good, especially when you are three (or four). He was totally excited.

"Do you want to help bake your birthday cake?"

"Yeah! Yes! Yummy!" This was too good to be true. Mom was usually a tad fussy about making a mess in the kitchen, especially with a mixer.

So we marched down to the kitchen and started mixing up that cake. We had a birthday breakfast while the cake cooled, and he was thrilled to be able to frost it all by himself and put in the *four* candles. This was the best birthday ever.

I called my husband at work.

"Hey, um, guess what? Today is Nick's birthday! Do you want to come home for lunch? We are having birthday cake with *four* candles on it. . . ."

"Hmmm, that is unexpected. I can't be there, but let me wish him a happy day. And good luck with this!"

My husband has known me for many years and somehow did not seem surprised by the whole development. He understands that desperation is the mother of invention (or something like that).

So we had chocolate birthday cake even before we had lunch. (Will wonders never cease on this magical day??) Then—and I am not kidding about this—he took two bites of cake, set down his fork, walked into the bathroom, and did it. Just like that. Number one and number two. Done. He was so proud of himself. I went in to cover Wiping 101, and then he was on his way—100 percent potty trained from that day forward. No accidents. No problems at night. Nada.

The roadblock was hurdled and he was on his way to the next challenge, whatever that might be. He believed he could do it, and suddenly he could.

Nick never asked about presents. He seemed very satisfied with how the day turned out. It was simply a happy birthday. We spent four months saying "Ixnay the Irthdaybay" to others when the subject came up. We informed friends and family that he was now "four," and people chuckled at the story. They may have raised their eyebrows, but I didn't care. We celebrated again in July while visiting family out of state, since they had not been there for the "big day." He received presents then, which must have seemed like a bonus. I am happy to report that we have stayed true to the calendar since then.

As his mother, I am still troubled that I bent the truth, even if the end seemed to justify the means. Can I call it a fib? Does that make it okay? When I come clean, do I have to include the times I imposed Mommy's Daylight Savings Time and changed all the clocks in the house to make everyone go to bed an hour early? I do try to live by a policy of truth, even when it is hard. I know that our children do as we do, not as we say, so I try to be a good role model of truth telling and other such matters.

Now my son has grown into the most honest person I've ever met at any age. Someday I will personally tell him the story. And when I do tell him about that birthday long ago, I hope he will hear these truths: sometimes in life, the power to believe you *can* do something is more powerful than the actual facts, ingenuity can make the long haul easier to bear, and maybe that cake can be a powerful motivator when the going gets rough. If someday he has the privilege to raise a fine son like himself, I hope he will understand why we do what we do.

Because somewhere between the mixing bowl, the oven, the calendar, and the candles lies the truth that we can succeed at any goal—if we just believe that today is the day we can do it.

♡

The Chase

By Gabrielle F. Descoteaux
as told to John J. Lesjack

Some days are diamonds. Some days are stones. Thursday, May 5, 1949, was a diamond of many carats that my family remembers with glee.

I was watching for the mailman's afternoon delivery because my government check was due. My spirits were high, but not because of the good weather. The check meant that I'd get our canned goods for the month, and I was happy because for the first time since my husband died, I had some canned foods left over from last month. Meats, milk, and bread would be picked up as needed, but I also had some coins in my purse. As a widow with six children, it took ingenuity, creativity, and discipline to balance my income with my outgo in those days. Plus, with children around all the time, I often had distractions that kept me from getting depressed.

While preparing dinner in the kitchen, I could look out the side window and see my sons playing baseball. Their father would have been proud. He was passionate about baseball. This was our first spring without him. I could look out the front window and see my girls playing "keep-away" on the front lawn with children from the neighborhood. I could also look down our long, rutted driveway and see the mailbox by the side of the road. The red flag was up because I had some bills going out. Distances between houses were great and made for good playing areas for children. True, we had a dirt road, no sidewalk, and no streetlight, but you can't have everything.

"Mom? Will you play with me today?" asked Mary, my seven-year-old blond child. She stood beside me in the kitchen.

"Honey, I'm watching for the mailman while I get dinner ready. If he brings my check, then I need to get some tuna fish at the store for the macaroni and cheese we're having tonight."

"You haven't played with me for a long time," Mary pouted. I tied the back of her dress before I gently sent her outside to join her older sisters.

I was mentally listing what I would need at the store after I went to the bank with my check. I needed to provide baked goods for church on Sunday, school lunches for my kids, new toothbrushes, and more. Everything had to last a month. This was the best I had felt since my husband had died six months ago. When I realized we were surviving, and that there would be another check next month, I felt like dancing.

Something moved out on the street and caught my eye. I looked out the front window. The flag was down and a vehicle was moving away from the mailbox. The stove was off, so I untied my apron, hung it on the hook, and walked out to get the mail.

When Mary saw me, she ran over and grabbed the mail out of the box. Then she ran and hid behind our front bushes. "Mary Jeannine, you naughty girl! You give me that mail right now!" I

shouted. The other girls stopped playing. They knew Mary Jeannine was in deep trouble. They watched me walk quickly over to
the bushes. But Mary wasn't there. She had run over to hide
behind the white birch tree. "I see you, Mary, and I want my
check!" I walked even more quickly over to the birch tree, only
to see Mary run to the back of the house. I jogged after her. Her
sisters were giggling and running behind me.

I chased my blond daughter across the backyard. Mary ran onto
the lot next door where the boys were playing baseball. I ran after
her. By now the other children were cheering and laughing, and
some were running with me. Neighbors came to their windows
or onto their porches to see what the ruckus was all about. They
stayed to smile and chuckle.

With her blonde hair flying behind her, Mary ran down the
first baseline and then out to the street. I followed. Cars slowed
down or stopped. Mary cut to her left, and then to her right. I ran
faster and closed in. She ran across third base and across home
plate, and that's where I caught her and lifted her off her feet. I
had the mail but I had lost my breath. I may have only been
thirty-three, but I wasn't used to that much running. Mary was
laughing, and I was never too tired to give my little girl a hug.

"I only had time for the one game," I told her.

"That was fun," Mary said.

I put my oldest daughter in charge of the others, drove to the
bank and the store, picked up our supplies, and drove home. That
night, over dinner of macaroni and cheese with fresh tomatoes,
tuna, and crushed, buttered crackers on top, we laughed about
the chase.

Then my oldest son, John, said, "Mom, after dinner, will you play baseball with us? You're an awesome base runner!"

High praise from an eleven-year-old!

When I brought out the red Jell-O for dessert, Mary Jeannine said, "Mom, that was the best macaroni and cheese we ever had!" And everyone laughed.

♡

Baby Book Bloopers

By Terri Elders

Each time my toddler son, Steve, uttered a new word—
"toast," "car," "ball"—I faithfully dragged out his baby
book and recorded it on the page entitled "Wonderful Words."
My eyes would then stray to the adjacent page headed "First
Complete Sentence." I remembered Mom saying mine was, "See
the moon."

I wondered what amazing observation Steve would make. My
fingers already itched to capture his exact words. I anticipated
the descriptive paragraph I'd compose, detailing the circumstances, the time, the place, the sights, sounds, and smells.

I knew from very recent experience that as a teen I had blushed
and rolled my eyes when Mama would recount my own early
years. But now that I'd reached young adulthood and had a child
of my own, I prodded her for more stories every chance I could. I
wanted to ensure that when Steve reached a similar age, his own
milestones would be at his fingertips.

It took just a minor leap of imagination to picture an adult
Steve displaying his baby book to his wife or even his own

grandchildren. I pictured him praising me for being such a faithful amanuensis. "My mom was the best!"

Well into his second year, Steve gushed and gurgled new words daily. His vocabulary expanded so quickly that I had to resort to entering the words on the margins of "Wonderful Words." But when it came to actual sentences, I'd hesitated to record such simple commands as "Me go now," or "Want milk." I wanted more for posterity. So I patiently waited for what I knew would be perceptive commentary, something as profound as "See the moon." I didn't want Steve shortchanged in the memory department.

When he was nearing two and a half, his dad and I took him on his first excursion to Marineland of the Pacific, a wonderful oceanarium in nearby Palos Verdes. Throughout the day I hovered over him, hoping for an utterance that I could at last classify as "First Complete Sentence." That page had remained blank far too long, and I was eager to tackle the next milestone.

Steve giggled at the antics of the dolphins, marveled at the seals and sea lions, gaped at Bubbles the Whale, but mumbled no more than an occasional "funny" or "big."

As the afternoon drew to a close, we went into the gift shop. Even that nook was lined with miniature aquariums featuring strange and exotic sea creatures from all over the world, showcased in their natural environments.

While I debated whether I should purchase a Bubbles shot glass embossed with the slogan "A Whale of a Drink" or settle for a set of postcards featuring the so-called flying fish, Steve wandered a few feet away to stare at a baby octopus that had emerged from behind a chunk of coral. No more than six inches long, it unfurled its tentacles, then drew them up tightly. Over and over again. Steve stared as if hypnotized, as the denizen of the deep repeated its rhythmic movements.

A minute later he shouted his first complete sentence—not merely an observation, but an inquiry. And everybody in the gift shop roared in appreciation. But my cheeks flamed.

When we got home, I dragged out the blue bound book and recorded Steve's blue-hued words. There they remain today: "Mama, Daddy, what the hell is that?"

The Gazing Ball

By Colleen Ferris Holz

I am a book junkie. After I became a mother, true to form, I relied on books to find answers to solve parenting questions, often related to discipline techniques. I was temporarily comforted by the suggestions I found. The advice from the so-called experts is so straightforward and logical when the kids are peacefully asleep tucked in their beds, but in the throes of daytime parenting, the suggestions learned are drowned out by feelings of frustration and worry. Yet in spite of parenting challenges and mistakes made, I have learned more enduring motherhood lessons that have come from more surprising sources. The insight might be subtle, often sprouting up organically right from the messes.

One September morning my sons, Hayden, four, and Samuel, almost two, and I were picking tomatoes from our garden on the side of our house.

"Only pick the red ones," I told Hayden after he had plucked three green ones.

Distracted for a moment, I turned my attention back to Samuel. I saw him standing in the shrub bed directly in front of our neighbor's house, holding a ball.

Wait a minute—a ball? I thought, with a split-second's worth of panic.

My "Nooooo!" came out too late, just as I saw Samuel drop the pink iridescent ball—like he expected it to bounce—into the stone-lined bed. The gazing ball was smashed into pieces.

Both boys, of course, wanted to explore the debris. "Don't touch the glass because you could cut yourself," I somehow managed to admonish calmly. The sound track in my head, however, was a stream of swearwords.

How are Nancy and Brad going to react to this? We don't know them as well as our other neighbors. What if they turn hostile toward us? What if that cheesy-looking ball was a cherished gift from a relative?

I scooped up Samuel and scurried into the house to get a trash bag. As I picked up tiny bits of glass between the stones, I thought how this was fitting bad karma for me. All the distain I've felt against lawn ornaments—this type in particular—resulted in this cosmic payback.

I never understood the purpose of those glass balls. I had always felt that they looked like a gaudy focal point against the garden or landscaping the homeowners had put time and money into designing. It was like sticking a neon "EAT" sign across a still life painting. If there is gazing to be done, shouldn't it be at the flowers, trees, or even the grass instead of at the distorted image reflected in a shiny ball?

The accident happened in the morning when my neighbors were at work. I felt confident that I retrieved most, if not all, of the glass shards out of the bed. I put a note on their front door and left a message on their answering machine offering to pay for the ball or replace it with a new one.

I had done all I could at that point. The broken glass was safely in the trash can. Yet, for the rest of the day, those flashy coral-pink smashed bits kept cutting through my thoughts.

Of course, I needed to vent to someone, so I called my friend Lisa. Samuel misbehaved during the conversation, so I promptly put him in a time-out. Lisa didn't have any words of comfort for me. She and her husband had chosen not to have kids. She probably muttered a prayer of gratitude after she hung up.

Lisa and Steve get along with all their neighbors. What if I just blew a chance at creating a friendship with ours because I didn't watch Samuel closely enough? Sure, they might be polite to me about it, but behind closed doors they'll be calling me that rotten mom who doesn't watch her kids!

Later in the day, the boys played on a train they created with kitchen chairs. One of them retrieved a Coke out of the refrigerator to give as a refreshment to their stuffed animal passengers in the dining car. The can rolled off a chair, fell, and burst open. We all wiped up the soda off the floor and the legs of the kitchen table and chairs. As I was changing Samuel's diaper, Hayden pulled a chair across the kitchen to retrieve his bank, which was on top of the refrigerator. The bank fell, its latch came open, and coins rained to the floor.

What else could fall or break today?

"I just wanted to count my coins," Hayden whined.

"Well, you could have asked for my help getting them down!" I grumbled.

It didn't stop there, of course. Like a caffeinated squirrel, Hayden ran around the house and climbed the living room furniture. By the time two ineffective time-outs were completed, my calm discipline approaches gave way to snarling and yelling.

When my husband, Gary, returned home from work, he found a quieter home. Desperate times had called for resorting to the crutch: the television. The boys were watching a show, while I was lying down in the bedroom to attempt to relieve the pounding over my eyes.

After dinner the boys played together well, and I felt like I was starting to recover. I was ready to apologize profusely to my neighbors when they returned home from work and head out to a garden store to buy a suitable replacement bauble for them.

Next, it was time to persuade the kids to pick up toys before bedtime. My approach: asking them over and over, each time progressively louder. Gary's method, in a voice resembling Mister Rogers, was to say, "Let's see who can pick up the most toys in ten minutes!" Defeated, I watched them scamper around enthusiastically retrieving toys.

Yeah, it's easy to be Mr. Positive and Patient when you haven't spent a whole day with these two! (Those glass splinters apparently weren't out from under my skin yet.)

I foolishly started sorting through some items in the toy room because it was getting crowded with too many toys. When Gary and the boys caught me trying to discard a dilapidated old toy that the kids had been ignoring, they ganged up on me, wanting to save the toy.

"That's it!" I yelled. "You *obviously* don't need *me* around here to get all of this cleaned up. I'm outta here!"

I put on my running shoes and left. Teeth clenched, mind and heart racing, I walked and walked. I felt the heavy weight of the parenting guilt you feel when you know that your ugly self had crept out from the shadows and hung around just a little too long.

A parenting book passage then came to mind—its timing too late—and scolded me: "Kids will mimic the words and behavior they see."

I thought about what it would be like to not turn around, to just keep going. Tears rolled down my cheeks. I was glad it was dusk and most people had gone inside.

I walked for blocks but turned back toward home after I stopped crying. I recognized a heavyset man walking toward the start of the block where I live. It was Brad, our neighbor.

"Nice night for a walk," he said. I had never seen him out walking before.

I agreed with a weak smile.

"Don't worry about that thing. I always hated it anyway."

I couldn't hold back a small laugh, but I insisted that we'd make amends to them anyway.

"Forget about it. Nancy and I really enjoy watching your boys have fun," he said, with a warm sincerity that reassured me and somehow communicated that I didn't have to protest further.

Brad continued on his walk, while I headed for home. I looked up at the sky, feeling humbled. I was reminded of renewable resources accessed not from a book but from within myself—self-forgiveness, resilience, and gratitude for my healthy, happy boys.

Yes, it had been a bad day. Yes, I had handled some things poorly. Yes, part of me still felt like walking away from home for a very long time. But a man who didn't know me very well had just given me permission to adjust my focus back to the bigger picture.

I breathed in the cool night air. While passing by my neighbor's front yard, I noticed they had crimson barberry shrubs in their bed just as we did. Nearby, deep burgundy red clematis climbed a white trellis between two clusters of orange tiger lilies.

In the periphery, the light from the toy room in our home glowed.

With no ugly ball as a distraction, I enjoyed the view.

♡

Teens Take Flight

By Tina Koenig

I t was a Friday morning in June, and I was looking forward to a month of sanity. My thirteen-year-old, Jason, and his best friend, Danny, were heading off to summer camp in North Carolina for thirty days, and I was in charge of airport transport.

We arrived at Hollywood–Fort Lauderdale International Airport as instructed, ninety minutes before takeoff. Because the boys were traveling on a charter flight, the airport staff let me escort them through security.

My son, Jason, a brown-haired angel of average build, made it through the scanners without a glitch, but my bracelet flagged the metal detector, and a fairy godmother with the National Transportation Safety Board (NTSB) pulled me aside and scanned me with her magic wand.

Meanwhile, Danny, who could pass for Jason's twin except that he packs a bit more weight, passed through the machine, too. The alarm blared. I watched as Danny was quarantined in a makeshift holding pen squared off with poles and vinyl strapping. After a few minutes, an agent asked loudly, "Whose child is this?"

I didn't answer right away. I wasn't sure I wanted to claim him like baggage. "I'm the adult responsible for him," I offered.

"We have to do a search," an NTSB agent said. "We need you to watch."

One of the agents grabbed a plastic bin. He asked me to step over to where they had corralled Danny. Danny removed two silver necklaces. He took off a belt and a watch. The watch face was the size of a personal pan pizza. The boy was so heavily laden with metal you could've sunk him for an artificial reef.

"Your pockets please," another agent said. From the depths of his pockets Danny brought forth a bundle of keys (at least enough to unlock the hearts of every girl south of Atlanta); several packages of guitar strings; quarters, dimes, nickels, and pennies; three football-shaped fishing weights; and a knife. Wisely, the agent confiscated the knife.

Meanwhile, inside the x-ray scanner, Danny's bag was attracting attention.

"Where are these kids going?" I heard someone ask.

Yet another NTSB worker approached me. "Ma'am, we need you to step over here."

I asked Jason to keep his eyes on Danny. An NTSB agent placed Danny's black canvas backpack on a separate table.

"Are they going camping?" the man asked. "There's some sort of spike in here."

I attempted to reach into the bag.

"You can't touch it until it's cleared," he says. "Right now it's the property of the federal government."

I got a visual of the last scene in *Raiders of the Lost Ark*, the one showing the Ark of the Covenant forever misfiled in government warehouse catacombs. I wondered if that was where all the tweezers and bottles of liquid more than three ounces ended up.

Danny and Jason joined me. We watched as two men started pulling the contents out of Danny's carry-on bag: small boxes of kosher dry cereal, half-eaten and unopened chocolate bars, handfuls of twenty-dollar bills, more change, a small amplifier for his guitar, triple-A batteries, a CD player and headphones, and three rolls of duct tape. We idled for a few moments over the duct tape.

I asked, "Danny . . . why do you need duct tape at camp?"

"It's good for closing wounds," he replied. "It sticks better than Band-Aids."

I took a minute. I wondered why the Band-Aid people hadn't thought of marketing duct tape.

"I'm sure it's great for gunshot wounds," I said.

The NTSB agent stepped back. "Does he have a gun in here?"

"GUM!" I say to the agent. "We were talking about GUM!"

As I pondered the imponderable uses for duct tape, the agent pulled out a six-inch-long iron railroad spike, the sort of dangerous, pointy object people objected to, the kind of thing used to kill, say, a vampire.

"This doesn't look like it's for a tent," the agent said.

I rolled my eyes. "Danny," I paused to take a breath. "Why do you have a railroad spike in your carry-on bag?"

He returned a blank stare and said, insightfully, "I don't know."

"Does it have any sentimental value?" I asked. "Is it a lucky charm, a paperweight for the twenty-dollar bills? Basically, what I want to know is, is it expendable?" With thirty minutes to go before boarding, the railroad spike was my nemesis. It was threatening my perfect summer.

"Throw it out," I told the agent. But he didn't. He had a better idea. He called his supervisor, a very wise and confident individual. He picked up the spike. He knew his team had dutifully confiscated every sewing kit and plastic container of explosive hair gel. He turned the spike over in his hands. He shrugged his shoulders. "I don't see why it can't go on board."

There were only two words that could adequately characterize my reaction: *shock* and *awe.*

I took matters into my own hands and confiscated the spike. I stared down the NTSB agents. Then I asked Danny a critical, decisive security question—one upon which the safety of air passengers depended, perhaps the security of the nation.

"Did you pack the change, duct tape, amplifier, and all those kosher-for-Passover chocolate bars yourself, or did someone ask you to carry those aboard the aircraft?"

The NTSB people glowered at me.

"Mom, stop embarrassing me!" my son said forcefully. "What's wrong with you? Are you trying to get us into trouble? Why can't you be normal like other mothers?" He looked at the NTSB people. "Just ignore her," he said. "She's crazy."

I was used to this. I tucked the six-inch spike deeper into my purse, because now it symbolized all things bureaucratic and brainless. I walked the boys to the gate and saw them off. As I waited for the plane to push away from the terminal, I couldn't help thinking about how handy that spike would have been when I was thirteen and still afraid of vampires and things that go bump in the night.

Only God Can Make a Tree

By Cookie Curci

On Christmas day in households across America, there are fragrant blossoms, graceful white pines, blue spruce, Douglas fir, scotch pine, and silvertips gracing the family home.

Each of these trees is eagerly decorated by parents, grandparents, children, and newlyweds in their own distinctive and individual way, and each leaves a memory for the family to share. But few of these memories can compare to the one Mom gave us the year she built our family Christmas tree.

It was 1955, the era of "do-it-yourself" America, a time when every member of the household had caught the do-it-yourself fever—remodeling, redecorating, or revamping just about everything in the family home. Tool chests and workshop benches were filled to capacity with modern gizmos and gadgets for the home handyman and decorator. It was a time of great self-expression, competition, and creativity. If something was good, then the do-it-yourselfer thought he could make it better with a nail over here and a whack over there.

It was this mode of modern, independent thinking and self-expression that both possessed and spurred Mom on to create the family Christmas tree that season. For her birthday that year, Mom asked for and got her own high-powered speed drill from Dad, along with a thick do-it-yourself book. She used her new gift to reset the hinges on the screen door, realign the kitchen shelves, and install new knobs on the cabinet drawers. With these household successes under her belt, Mom decided to take her creativity one step further. With Christmas Eve just a few days off, Mom surprised us all by saying she was going to build a tree. Dad believed Mom was courting disaster in monkeying around with something so traditional and sacred, and he told her so.

Taking her trusty drill in hand, Mom proceeded to follow her newly created plans. She drilled a countless number of holes into a tall, round closet pole. Then on a brisk December morning, we happily hiked into the hills to help Mom gather tree branches for her project. Mom quickly set to work filling the holes she'd drilled into the pole. After long hours of trimming, shaping, and snipping, Mom called the family in to see her finished work. Mom's creation looked great.

That night, we all took part in decorating the newly made tree. We layered our new tree with garland, ornaments, lights, and tinsel. We went to bed that night happy and pleased with Mom's miraculous, ultramodern tree, believing we were soon to be the envy of the neighborhood.

The following morning we awoke and ran to the living room for another look. We were shocked and disappointed to discover that the once-glorious tree had dried up during the night. Its branches folded up tightly like a neatly closed umbrella. The ornaments, tinsel, and lights had all cascaded to the floor and lay in a heap at the bottom of the clump of branches.

We all stood and stared in bewildered silence. We looked at Mom, whose face was expressionless. We didn't know if she was about to laugh or cry. Her do-it-yourself handbook didn't have a page for this dilemma. Dad broke the silence with a chuckle that had an "I-told-you-so" ring to it. Suddenly we were all laughing— Mom the loudest. Dad put on his hat and coat and dashed out the door to the nearest tree lot and returned home with a suitable silvertip.

I can't remember much about the tree Dad brought home that Christmas Eve, but I'll always remember Mom's enthusiastic effort. Her tree might not have made it through the holidays, but the fun and memories she made for us that year will last a lifetime.

♡

Say That Again

By Ryma Shohami

It had been a summer to cherish: sunshine and dazzling blue skies, ice-cold lemonade, and perfect beach weather—unless you were conspicuously pregnant and resembled a beached whale, that is. And, as if a sixty-pound weight gain and ankles that an elephant would die for were not punishment enough, September, my last month, was one torturous heat wave.

The thrill of expecting my first child was wearing a little thin as I counted down the days to liftoff, as my husband had so quaintly taken to calling my due date. Finally, week forty ended, and on the morning of the first day of week forty-one, I naively placed my overnight case near the door and sat down with a magazine to wait for the contractions.

Three days later found me still pregnant and surrounded by an ever-increasing pile of magazines. My normally efficient husband was helpless in the face of my whining complaints. He opted for professional intervention and drove me to my gynecologist, who promptly sent me to the hospital for an ultrasound.

At the hospital, an argument ensued among the medical staff as to how far along I really was. The sight of two nurses, one technician, and two doctors not being able to reach a consensus did nothing to improve my mood.

They finally settled on thirty-six weeks, which completely unsettled me. I politely informed everyone that, although I respected their medical prowess, I absolutely refused to be pregnant for another four weeks. The technician frowned, but wisely decided to remain silent.

I gently explained that my mother had traveled from abroad to help me with the baby and that she could not hang around for another month. One of the doctors cleared his throat in an unsuccessful attempt to stop himself from laughing.

I then threatened to obtain an appropriate potion, squat in the field behind my house, and give birth the old-fashioned way. Possibly that very afternoon. Concluding that the heat and the shock had deranged me, the second doctor sent me home with instructions to return in three days.

This ritual of ultrasounds and disagreements continued for another ten days. When the baby finally decided to join the family, I was so unprepared that her announcement sent me down to the floor on all fours, panting in a way that no prenatal class had ever taught.

Three hours into labor, the attending doctor, whom I'd never seen before that afternoon, concluded that an episiotomy was just the ticket. The rotund midwife attending me immediately set up a ruckus, insisting that it would all be over in another ten minutes.

From your mouth to God's ears, I prayed silently.

The doctor argued that I had at least two hours to go. He was not a nice man, I concluded. Vaguely, I wondered if anyone agreed with anyone else about anything in this place. Suddenly, they both switched to Russian. Perhaps they didn't want to upset me with their bickering. I decided not to reveal just yet that I understood every word.

For the next several minutes, while I alternated between threatening to kill the next person who came near me and praying for a quick death, the doctor and midwife played one-upmanship, testily comparing their respective credentials and experience.

Did I need to hear curriculum vitae at a time like this?

The midwife stood her ground: no episiotomy. The doctor, sensing defeat, proceeded to throw a tantrum.

"If you think you know better than a doctor, go ahead and do it your way," he sulked. "I have other patients," he added, flouncing out of the room.

The midwife, not to be outdone, stormed out after him, shouting, "Twenty-five years, and not a single mishap! If anything happens to her, it's on your head!"

In the sudden silence—I was between contractions—my husband and I stared at each other, stunned at having been abandoned. Not understanding any Russian, he had no clue as to what had just transpired.

"What happened?" he whispered, still in shock.

"They had to leave," I finally managed to gasp, as another wave attacked my sanity.

"Where did they go?" he shouted in a panic.

"Coffee break!" I shrieked, panting and pushing.

My screams brought a flurry of nurses, one of whom, trying to pacify me, cooed reassuringly, "Sweetie, I'll give you coffee just as soon as this is all over."

Just then, the midwife waddled into the room.

"Aha! Exactly twenty minutes," she crowed delightedly as she caught the baby on my final push.

"Next time, could you be nicer to the doctor?" I whispered in perfect Russian, rendering her speechless for the first time that afternoon.

"Oh, honey," she finally recovered, "if I'd known you were one of us, I would never have let that hack near you in the first place."

"What's she saying?" my husband asked, all confused.

"She said the baby is beautiful," I said, too exhausted to translate for him.

"Well, of course she is. She looks like her mother," he said.

And I suddenly realized that all the frustrations and annoyances of the past two weeks, and all the pain and lunacy of the past four hours were already forgotten, because I was the mother he was talking about. And that mother now had a beautiful new baby who looked just like her. Can summer get any cooler?

Mom-ese

By Jill Sunshine

My mother speaks her own language. No, she is not the lone survivor of some far-off country, a visionary woman who strives to preserve the language of her ancestors. Rather, she is simply an inventor of her own words and phrases, which she sneakily incorporates into her native English, leaving her children no alternative than to think their Mom's English is the same as the Queen's English.

Apparently, Mom is no queen (except of her children's hearts).

I first discovered that I had additional vocabulary in my back pocket when spending the night at a friend's house. I wanted to compliment my friend on giving me my favorite kind of blanket, the kind with "bite-thee" on it.

"What's 'bite-thee'?" she asked, nose crinkled.

"You don't know what 'bite-thee' is?" I asked. I showed her the satin on the edge of the blanket and explained to her as though she were learning English. "We call this 'bite-thee,'" I said with more than a hint of superiority at teaching her something, as she was at least a year older than me, which is equivalent to a decade for a kid. Little did I know that the "We" in my statement referred to approximately four people, and all of them lived in my house.

Always looking to show off, I went home and told my mom how Christy did not even know what "bite-thee" was.

"That's because your brother made that word up," Mom said.

My brother? If he made it up, why was Mom always using it? "Feel the bite-thee," she would say. I even named my blanket-friend (you know, the kind like Linus had) "bite-thee." Wouldn't bite-thee be sad to learn that his name was a product of my brother's invention and not a tribute to his exceptional softness?

"When did he make that up?" I asked. *And why did you act like it's a word?* I added silently.

"He used to bite it, and we said he was biting the bullet. So we call it 'bite-thee.'"

Even in my youth, I suspected that there was some serious logic missing here. How is biting the soft part of a blanket like biting a bullet? Although I had never seen one, I was pretty sure that bullets were not soft. And how did it all mutate into one word, "bite-thee"? Were we suddenly Shakespearean, using "thee" to address a blanket? Despite Mom's explanation to absolve herself of having created that word, I was even more sure that she was guilty of unauthorized word fabrication. Evidence of the story indicated that the word was made up even before my brother could talk, back when all he did was bite.

I wondered with dismay how many other words that I used were the product of my mother's ingenuity. I observed her to try to figure it out. Some Mom-ese vocabulary was obvious. When my mother wanted the trash taken out, she would stand near the trash can and shout, "Trashola abenzola!" The rhyming nature of this phrase, and the hint of English in the word "trash," made me realize that it was a Mom Original phrase, and I cleverly never used it at anyone else's house. I knew I would sound stupid asking people if they have to "trashola abenzola" or if that was their sibling's job.

There were, of course, the curse words in Mom-ese. These words included but were not limited to "Zamu!" and "Hockamenah!" which she would shout when something landed on her foot, she touched something hot in the kitchen, or she saw me in the hallway and did not know I was home. To this day, Mom tries to say she was shouting "Zockamenah!" with a "Z" (I never, ever heard the "Z" sound). Quite frankly, the last letter of the alphabet does little to improve the lyrical nature of the cursing in her language, so Mom should just give up on that debate.

Mom had so many phrases that my little sister once made her a dictionary. I think it was a gift to honor Mom and her unique mothering techniques, but I also hoped she would learn the English equivalents to her invented ramblings.

Mom's love affair with Spanish further complicated the matter. In addition to inserting her invented words and phrases into her daily speech, she also inserted Spanish. I grew up helping Mom find her "bolsa" (she never said "purse"), and at night I slept with a "pilota." As Mom is constantly complimented by Spanish speakers for her impeccable accent (it is pretty good), I assumed her Spanish was similarly superb. Never assume anything with my mom. She is nothing, if not consistently inconsistent with a great accent.

She was right about "bolsa" meaning "purse," but "pilota" does not mean "pillow." No, "pilota" means a "female pilot." All those times Mom told me to grab her female pilot and put it in the trunk of the car for a camping trip, or to take my sleeping bag and female pilot with me to spend the night at a friend's house seemed funny once I learned that she had simply assumed that "pillow" would sound like "pilota" in Spanish. I marvel that Mom is so good with languages that when she messes one up, she does manage to at least say something else in the same language.

I still remember the confusion I felt when I read the word "crapola" in a novel in high school. I had lumped that word into the Mom-ese category, but here it was in a novel written by the inhabitant of another continent. Had I miscategorized this word, or was Mom's language spreading? I guessed the former, but the latter intrigued me. What would it take for Mom to change English as we know it?

One truth was clear: as a child, my inability to separate the world of my mother from the actual world reveals her importance to my upbringing. She was my world, spending so much time and energy on mothering. Not being able to separate the whole wide world with the world of my mother's burgeoning imagination was a "problem" I feel honored to have. By creating words, Mom was creating meaning. In an indirect way, she was showing me that I could say and be whoever I wanted. Her imagination was not limited by the words in the English dictionary; similarly, the bounds for what I could feel, experience, and become in my life had no limits. She let me know that the world was a canvas on which to write the tale of my life, and I had every chance to create the exact life, the exact meaning that I wanted.

My mother is the ultimate "Momola." Whatever she says, and in whatever language she says it, she speaks with love.

New
Beginnings

Magnetic New Beginnings

By Connie K. Pombo

I t was June 5, 2001—the day our new refrigerator was due to arrive. Before the appliance technicians parked their truck in the driveway, I hastily shoved the leftover refrigerator magnets, the family calendar, and photos from the front of our fifteen-year-old Kenmore into a file folder. The refrigerator of my dreams was about to make its debut—the sleek black side-by-side came complete with a water and ice dispenser.

The first time I heard the ice go *chink, chink, chink* against the glass tumbler, I cheered, "Yeah, no more ice cube trays!" In the middle of the night, I tiptoed into the kitchen just to watch the water dispenser light glow. I was in refrigerator heaven!

Two weeks later, my sleek new refrigerator started collecting new material: a magnet or two, report cards, birthday photos, and party invitations. After a long family vacation in Florida, I brought back a sand dollar magnet that held the invitation to Jon's open house at high school and Jeremy's parents' day at college. The giant new machine started to fill up, and the family calendar was once again front and center. The refrigerator felt like a part of the family again.

And just when I thought we couldn't put another piece of paper or another magnet on the refrigerator door, Jon's acceptance letter from college arrived. He would be going to Grove City College in Pennsylvania. Our baby was leaving home—it couldn't be! Where did the time go?

For weeks—no, months—the letter hung on the refrigerator door along with a letter from the president of the college welcoming all new freshmen. Later it was replaced with a packing list of all the "needed" dorm items: refrigerator, television, microwave, and a George Foreman grill. *Was he going away to study or to play house?*

The day we dropped Jon off at college, we helped him carry his portable white refrigerator up the dorm steps and filled its tiny doors with Gatorade. It was then that I realized he wasn't coming back home. *Why should he? He had a refrigerator of his own!* I fought back the tears and swallowed hard to keep from drowning in grief.

"Mom, where did you put my sheets and towels?" Jon demanded, as he entered the small dorm cubicle that reeked of Lysol.

"I put them in the closet with your other things," I shouted from the other side of the room.

"Why did you do that?" he countered.

I felt a tear slip down my cheek—then another, and another, until they formed a puddle on the gray-streaked linoleum floor.

Jon sat on the bed beside me and whispered, "Mom, PLEEEEZE don't cry." I felt his strong arms wrap themselves around me while he softly patted me on the shoulder—the way I had consoled him so many times through the years. Finally, Jon broke the silence and said, "C'mon, let's all go out to eat. I'm hungry!"

I knew Jon was trying to divert my attention, and it worked until the moment we had to say our "final" good-byes. Jon hugged me and said, "Mom, promise me you won't start crying again when you get in the car!"

Jon waved a confident good-bye. And as soon as we pulled out of the parking lot, I broke my promise. I cried—no, *sobbed*—for the next fifty-two miles on the Pennsylvania turnpike. Mark, my hubby of thirty years, didn't even try to console me. He just turned up the volume on the radio to drown out my sniffling.

When we arrived back home, I did the first thing Jon always did: I opened up the refrigerator door. There lay Jon's half-eaten turkey sandwich in a crumpled-up wrapper and an empty can of Coke—remnants of his last day at home. I slumped into the kitchen chair and the tears flowed freely.

For days, the refrigerator stood as a reminder of the once-full life we had with our boys: soccer tournaments, summer mission trips, orthodontic appointments, and family vacations. Now all that remained was a clean, sleek refrigerator—the one I always wanted. I left the refrigerator door open—just like Jon—and wandered into his bedroom and cried more tears on his pillow. The house was empty and the sound of laughter was gone. I was facing the empty nest!

A week after Jon left for college, I got an invitation in the mail for "Ladies' Night Out" at our church. The invitation was so clever: it was a refrigerator magnet in the form of a cappuccino cup with the words "Café-O-Laugh-Day." But I wasn't in the mood for laughter and tossed the magnetic invitation into the trash.

Moments later I started to prepare dinner and stared at the front of the refrigerator. It was clean, free of magnets, and—at last—no clutter. *Just the way I always wanted, right?*

I retrieved the invitation from the garbage—complete with orange peels and coffee grounds glued to the front—and slapped it on the refrigerator door. I smiled. And for a second, I thought the refrigerator winked back. The sleek black door was a clean slate—a new beginning to do all the things I had put on hold while our boys were growing up. We built precious memories with our sons that paved the way for them to start a new life on their own. Now it was my turn! I glanced over at the half-written book proposal lying on the desk. It had remained there for three years while I waited for uninterrupted time to write. There were plans for a garden we never planted and brochures for a cruise we never took—all dreams waiting to be fulfilled.

It's been three years since our "baby" left for college and I finally finished the book. The garden is complete and we continue to add a variety of new flowers each year. And the cruise—well—it was a gift, a celebration of thirty years of marriage!

Today the refrigerator door remains clean of clutter except for *one* magnet with a quote by Thomas Fuller: "Leftovers in their less visible form are called memories; stored in the refrigerator of the mind and the cupboard of the heart."

It wasn't the empty nest that I was facing, but a time of "magnetic" new beginnings!

If By Some Miracle . . .

By Michelle L. Miller

T wo months before my wedding I was diagnosed with cancer. "Don't marry me," I told Bill, hoping that he'd run
from the catastrophic doom that I was sure would be my fate.
"You're not getting rid of me that easily," he replied and reined me
in for a kiss. At thirty-three years old and a newlywed, infertility
was the result of chemotherapy. Our dream of having a family in
the old-fashioned way was forever kidnapped without a ransom
note.

One day at work, as I exited a bathroom stall, a coworker
whom I hardly knew asked me if I'd be able to have children since
I had cancer, and if I couldn't, would my husband divorce me. My
body clenched and I tried to hide my offended expression while
I readjusted my wig. That night, filled with embarrassment and
shame, I told Bill what had happened. I couldn't imagine my life
without children. "We never had a chance to have a baby," I
sobbed. "Maybe God has a better plan for us," he mused. I wasn't
so sure. After all, I had cancer. "The bottom line," Bill reminded,
"is that I love you—all of you—I'm not married to your ovaries,"
he chuckled. We talked about other parenting options, but by

then my head hurt from crying all day. I only half listened when the word "adoption" was mentioned, but Bill's smile was evident.

Eight years later, and with periodic maintenance chemotherapy, I found a new normal within the chaos and was successful in professional and academic endeavors beyond even my own expectations. Most people never knew I had cancer, and life moved forward in spite of it. After a while, diplomas and walls of trophies for my accomplishments couldn't inspire me to pump my body with more drugs to maintain a short leash on cancer. The true purpose of my life was again in question and my heart was heavy with unbearable sadness. One day in my doctor's office while we talked about new cancer drugs, I blurted, "I need to be a mother. I'm running out of good reasons to continue this fight." My doctor was dumbstruck. "I've never heard you say anything remotely close to giving up," he said.

My maternal instincts were both deeply primal and ingrained. Despite cancer I couldn't ignore my need any longer. I was raised in the 1970s with its blend of female empowerment and traditional norms. I could be the president of a company or the president of the United States. But, I was told, unmistakably my true purpose would always be rooted in motherhood. Motherhood was simultaneously a woman's duty and a blessing; to not have children meant a sad and lonely old age. A year before Bill and I married we bought a big house and planned for two kids and one salary—his—so I could be a stay-at-home mom. Now everything seemed meaningless.

During the previous eight years I kept an adoption journal. My passionate letters to an anonymous child were therapeutic for me.

On some wishful level, I hoped that by writing my innermost desires, they might become a reality. As much as I needed to be a mother, there were moments when self-doubt loomed. Could I balance the toughest job in the world and cancer, too? True, there would be occasional challenges, but life is rarely smooth for anyone. A dedicated, loving mother with cancer had to be better than being an orphan. Bill never doubted my ability. "We're a team," he said, "and whatever happens, we'll handle it."

So with love and hope in our hearts, we made a spare bedroom into a nursery and began the open adoption process. On paper we were the ideal couple, but because I had chronic cancer we weren't perfect enough for adoption agencies. Even despite supportive documentation from three doctors about my prognosis and ability to raise a child to adulthood, we were rejected by adoption agencies. On occasion, my pride was rattled and I felt like a failure. Mostly, the refusals made me relentless in my quest. Some rejections were polite. Sometimes they were downright cruel. "Why would a birth mother choose you," said one adoption worker, "when there are so many healthy people that want to adopt?" Those words stung like a swarm of bees.

One day at a local supermarket I saw flyers about an adoption agency that I'd never contacted. I paced by the stack several times, undecided about whether to take one. Surely another rejection would be mine, I thought. "Believe," a voice inside me urged. I took one and raced home to phone the agency. We met the next day, and after explaining our situation, they welcomed us without hesitation. We were hopeful, but cautiously optimistic. Soon after, we completed our paperwork and submitted our portfolio for a birth mother to select us. Within weeks a young couple experiencing economic hardship and soon to have their third child, a boy, chose us. That December was a flurry of elated activity as we made several trips across the state to bond with the birth family. It seemed that our prayers had finally been answered. Gratitude filled our hearts, and I imagined how decades later I'd retell the miraculous story of God's power.

Three days after Christmas everything unraveled. Despite extreme poverty the couple did not want to put their child up for adoption. Our joy turned to numb silence. Because of travel and preparations for the baby, we hadn't made time to decorate our home for the holidays. Now the lack of a tree, mistletoe, or a hint of garland was a further expression of our loss. We were grief-stricken. I felt flattened, beyond tears, and wanted the pain to stop. I went to the nursery, gathered whatever I could, threw it all into the closet, and closed the bedroom door, unable to go inside that room again. I announced to Bill that I was through with adoption. I couldn't take another step in the journey. Defeated, I called the adoption agency to withdraw our interest. Our social worker encouraged me to be persistent. I halfheartedly agreed and expected nothing. The next day, I continued to stew about the situation. I knew that I had to find peace about the possibility of being childless but couldn't accept such a reality. In a few days the year would be over. I vowed to not take the emotional baggage of that year into the next.

Silently, I spoke with God and said that I was giving the entire matter over to him. It was clear that I was not in control. If by some miracle it was his will that I should be a mother, then it

would be so; if not, I'd try to find renewed purpose in a life with
chronic cancer.

That New Year's Eve we forced smiles and counted the seconds
to 2008. The next morning, we received a desperate telephone
call from the adoption agency. A healthy baby girl, born that
morning, was in need of adoptive parents. "She's yours," said
Vicky from the adoption agency, "Get to the hospital as fast as
you can!" During the six-hour car ride I felt my faith being tested
again. *God, I need you now*, I prayed. At the hospital, I pressed my
nose against the nursery window to see my daughter. As she slept,
her tiny body flinched and her brow furrowed under the bright
lights. Never had I seen pure innocence such as this. In that
moment, I vowed to love and protect her forever.

Passionate, powerful, unconditional love like I had never
known enveloped me like uncontrollable waves. A sense of peace
and wholeness fell upon my spirit as I cradled my baby and gazed
into her dark eyes. I needed her as much as she needed me. She
was mine . . . it was as though she had always been mine and
merely waited for the right time to come.

Wise beyond her eighteen years and already the mother of a
two-year-old boy, Christine, the birth mother, chose adoption as
a better option. She was a tall, hazel-eyed beauty with long,
brown hair. I never judged Christine for her life choices and she
never judged me for having cancer. We had only a few hours
together but conversation and trust came easily. "What will you
name her?" she asked me. "Elizabeth," I said. "She will always be
our little princess," I promised. Christine smiled and her shoulders relaxed.

From her hospital bed we hugged and thanked her for making our dream come true. She held her son in her lap and watched as Elizabeth was carried away to her new life. Our daughter will always know that Christine's decision to let her be adopted was a courageous, loving one.

Today, I still have cancer, but because of a mother's sacrifice and God's plan I have achieved my ultimate shining victory—I am now a mother.

Letting Go of
the Key

By Ferida Wolff

I am walking around the house on the eve of my son's wedding. This is a happy time. He is marrying a woman I love, who obviously loves my son. I know they will be happy together and I am enthusiastically looking forward to this celebration. Yet, nostalgia has overtaken me.

I remember holding my son moments after he was born. He worked so hard at lifting his head to see me. We looked into each other's eyes and I was captured. I knew I would love him forever. It was as if he had given me the key to a golden city, his care and well-being transferred to my hands. I accepted the key with gratitude and anxiety. Would I be able to fulfill the trust presented to me?

I see pictures in my mind of the three-year-old being pulled around in a wagon by his sister and her friend while he sits serenely snacking on a baked potato. I feel his tiny hand in mine as we walk down the street. He needed me then for the basics of life, and I felt privileged to be able to provide them. But the key was only on loan and I knew it.

I replay his first day at preschool when he wanted me to stay. I knew I was handing him back his key, temporarily. He was leaving me, reluctantly at first but eagerly soon after, and taking his first steps toward independence. Each day when he returned, the key was transferred back and we both felt a little easier.

I see him biking down the street on his first two-wheeler, his abundant brown hair blowing in the wind and independence shining on his face. I watch him going off to school with his friends with hardly a backward glance, and I remember how proud I was of him. He was growing up as he was meant to.

Over the years he chose to keep his key more often, returning it less frequently. But there was always that connection, the invisible thread that made us both keepers of the key. When trouble stuck, that thread thickened and we shared the responsibility the key demanded. There was no one to blame when he fell off the climbing gym at nine and broke his wrist. Risking is an important part of life's experience. For a while, though, as I made sure he received the proper medical care and comforted him when he hurt, I held the key. As soon as his wrist healed, he was back in possession and back climbing.

When he was diagnosed with diabetes after a bout with the flu at sixteen, no matter how I wanted to protect him and spare him from the disease, he was the one who had to care for himself. He took over his daily shots and monitored his blood sugar. I tried to hold on to the key by planning his meals and keeping on top of his monitoring, but he wouldn't let me. He had too much living to do and was often gone: on weekend camping trips with his scout troop, on school trips, overnight at his friends. He knew that he was in charge, so I backed off.

As I wander in and out of rooms, his bedroom still loaded with his boyhood furniture, the toy room stocked with his favorite games, the den where he often fell asleep while watching television, I question my motivation. I have been only a peripheral part of his life since his college years really, but I still felt that bond that was evident at the beginning of his life. *Am I trying to hold on to him?* I wonder. *Am I being the cartoon mother-in-law?*

My friend said that she felt the same nostalgia when her son married. It wasn't anything against his fiancée I was feeling but a shift of allegiance. Now he will be consulting his wife on the major questions of life. He will present me with his choices and not his quandaries. His father and I will no longer be his next of kin, and his birth family will be less important to him than his newly formed family.

I am glad. I've seen the results when a man was not able to make that shift. His children always felt second best and his wife came up short in any comparison. It does not make for a secure family. What he didn't realize was that his first family was the background for his chosen family. They would always love him. He didn't need to prove it. He was just never able to claim his own key.

My nostalgia tour is over. I mentally wrap the thread around the jewelry box that holds the rings for tomorrow's ceremony, the rings my son had entrusted to me to hold until his wedding day. I do it carefully and deliberately so it will not tangle. My love for them both makes letting go of the key not a reluctant duty but a sacred rite of motherhood.

Standing at West Point

By Judy Wilson as told to Peggy Frezon

er cap and gown lay crumpled on the family room couch. Partially eaten blue and white frosted cake sat on the kitchen counter. And now, the very day after high school graduation, I stood in the driveway preparing to take my daughter off to the United States Military Academy at West Point.

My husband, Tony, waited by the van. "You ready?" he called into the house, gathering the family for the trip. I climbed into my seat as he slid behind the wheel and our two sons piled into the back. I watched Elissa slip out of the house, her long blond hair loose at her shoulders, denim shorts and tan Birkenstocks suggesting a day at the beach. Instead, her days would be spent marching and drilling under the hot sun. Just the thought made my feet ache for her.

"That's quite an ambition," I'd said when she first mentioned her desire to attend West Point. But inside, I had hoped it was just a romantic idea that would soon fade away.

Of course, I was proud when, later, she was accepted. West Point required top grades, physical fitness, and a congressional appointment. She made the honor roll and was the captain of her track team. And what a tribute when the congressman selected her! Obviously he had seen something special in her. But she wasn't ready for this, was she?

Elissa tossed her luggage on the seat. I remembered my friends joking about needing U-Hauls for all their kids' college gear. Elissa had one blue duffel bag. One. That was all she was allowed to bring.

Last week I'd watched her pack that bag. Her favorite floral dress remained in the closet. I picked up a stylish, strappy leather sandal and turned it over and over in my hands. "Are you sure you're going to be okay wearing a uniform every day?" I asked.

I thought, too, of her living in a stark dorm room. Nothing would be allowed on the shelves and walls at West Point. Even her threadbare, stuffed bunny, the one she'd had since she was a baby, would stay behind.

We drove mostly in silence, each of us deep in our own thoughts. When we arrived at West Point, we followed a winding driveway lined with evergreens and stone walls. Old granite buildings, military Gothic architecture, towers, and parapets stood like sentinels on the banks of the Hudson River. Everything was neat and orderly, formal and regimented. Full of tradition and honor, in every sense a fortress.

But wait! This was my little girl. I had dressed her in pink and tied ribbons in her hair. The girl who used to run into the house with a gap-toothed smile and a handful of dandelions as golden as her hair. I used to watch her carry her favorite doll in a basket over her arm. I hadn't raised her to carry a gun. Or, God forbid, to die for her country. I thought of the mandatory five years of active military service required after graduation and shuddered. She wasn't ready for any of this!

We walked slowly across the crowded campus to Eisenhower Hall, a large, modern brick building. An orientation briefing was being held in the auditorium. A colonel, striped medals over his pocket, stood before the crowd. He told us about the classes: Close Quarter Combat, Survival Swimming, Boxing. Combat? Survival? If only she was simply taking English and Biology.

I shifted anxiously until the speeches were over. The colonel's next words were clear. "You now have forty-five seconds to say good-bye to your cadet."

Seconds?! We all hugged Elissa. I held on tight. "I love you," I said. I wanted to cling, to hold her back, but the precious seconds ticked away.

"Love you, Mom," she said as she picked up her duffel bag. I watched her move down the aisle, to the front of the auditorium, and out a side door. Wait!

She was gone.

Now there was nothing to do but wait for the swearing-in ceremony. I wouldn't get to see my daughter in person or talk to her again that day. Even later, basic training rules only allowed her two brief phone calls home.

We walked outside between the stone bridges connecting the buildings. I caught a glimpse of a squad of cadets learning to march. They had already been transformed, dressed in black shorts, grey T-shirts, and black shoes. Was Elissa there? She's not *ready for this!* I thought again.

Soon we assembled on a grassy field where we would wait until the swearing-in ceremony. The ache to see my daughter swelled.

I knew there was little chance I could pick her out of the thousands of similarly clad cadets. But maybe, if I got up close before they marched off to the day's final ceremony. . . .

I went up to another parent on the green and asked, "Please, do you know where the cadets come out before the ceremony?"

He gave me a knowing look and asked for her company and platoon.

"B-4," I replied. It didn't mean anything to me yet, but I had it memorized.

He smiled kindly, directing me toward Washington Hall. "The platoons come out in alphabetical order," he explained. "So A . . . B . . . B will come out right there, through that sally port." He pointed to a beautiful stone archway built into the wings of the massive granite building.

"Oh, thank you!" My family and I rushed to a spot in the grass closest to the opening. I heard the cadence of marching feet, felt the hum of activity, and knew the cadets were just behind the wall. My eyes fixed on the sally port behind which I was told my daughter would be. A band began to play. My heart pounded twice as fast as the beat as I spotted the platoon, now dressed in white over gray, emerging beneath the arch. I tried to determine which cadet was Elissa. She was not in the first row or the second . . . the line moved forward, stopping to make a neat turn almost directly in front of me.

I could see them clearly now, each body, each face as they marched past with perfect rhythm. And then, there she was! Elissa! Straight posture, poised and proud. Long gray pants with a dark stripe, white short-sleeved shirt neatly tucked, white dress gloves, her hair pulled up into a bun at the back of her head. *Elissa, look! Here I am!*

But as she came near, her expression was intent, her eyes focused only on the platoon leader. She didn't see me.

I swayed, my legs giving out beneath me as my daughter marched out of sight. "Whoa, Judy, are you okay?" Tony steadied me with an arm around my shoulder.

I nodded, embarrassed, and took a deep breath. The cadets had marched by and Elissa hadn't seen me.

But just as quickly as that thought entered, a new thought crossed my mind. She hadn't seen me, but maybe that was how it should be. More important was what I had seen in her eyes. She was focused and fully immersed in her duty. She had stepped into this new chapter, heart and soul. Yes, she was ready for this.

All along I was the one who wasn't ready.

Before we went home, we stood together, solemnly watching the swearing-in ceremony at Trophy Point, near an impressive amphitheater on the banks of the sparkling Hudson River. The peaceful blue ribbon of water wound between two humpbacked mountains in the distance. I heard the colonel's words spread over the gathering. "New cadets, raise your right hand and repeat after me. . . ."

I smiled proudly, knowing that Elissa stood tall among the sea of gray, taking her oath. This was something she'd wanted and prepared for, heart and soul. I'd still miss her, but Elissa was ready for this, and so was I.

When the ceremony ended, Elissa marched away. We lingered until the drumbeats were only an echo in the distance, but I could still hear them, feel them, in my heart.

The Eggcellent Mother

By Emily Parke Chase

My mother and father were married for almost forty years before illness led to my mother's death. Dad handled the loss well, but it was obvious to me that he was lonely, so when he announced that he was thinking of remarrying, I was delighted. My brothers and I gathered from various corners of the country to meet the prospective bride.

Poor Andy was nervous, hoping we would approve of her. If you think it is hard to meet the parents of your intended, imagine having to meet the children and grandchildren of your spouse-to-be! When she walked into the living room where all of us were seated, comparisons were inevitable. Where my mother was tall, Andy was not. My mother had long, dark brown hair, while Andy's hair was short with red highlights. My mother was a wonderful cook, but Andy, as we learned, had little experience in the kitchen.

We made awkward attempts at conversation before moving to the dining room for dinner. Then, just as my oldest brother pulled the hot lasagna out of the oven, a bump caused the pan to slip from his hand and he dropped it on the floor. Suddenly eggs, melted cheese, tomato sauce, and pasta noodles slithered across the floor. As the lasagna flew into pieces, our tension shattered, too. We all laughed as we grabbed spatulas, bowls, sponges, and rags to collect the hot, lavalike eruption. Yes, we salvaged enough to serve with salad for supper.

At the end of the meal, I gave Andy a quick hug of approval, saying, "All I ask is that you appreciate and love my father as much as we do." In the years since, she has met and far exceeded that requirement.

One night shortly after their marriage, my stepmom made a large batch of egg salad and tucked it into the refrigerator to cool in preparation for a ladies' tea the following day. Then she and Dad headed to bed. Dad, as usual, promptly fell asleep, but Andy lay awake. Somehow the salad didn't seem right. Was it too runny? Not enough eggs? Had she added too much mayonnaise?

After an hour or two of lying awake wondering what to do about the salad, Andy crept out of bed and got dressed. Dad stirred sleepily and asked what time it was.

"It's 2:00 AM," she replied.

"Where are you going?"

Andy replied, "The egg salad is too runny. I'm going to the store to buy more eggs and make a new batch."

"At two in the morning?! Oh, Joan, come to bed!"

Andy humphed and tapped her chest. "Hey, that was wife number one. This is wife number two!"

Dad rolled over on his side and muttered, "Well, going-shopping at 2:00 AM is just the crazy sort of thing my Joanie would have done."

Andy beamed and headed to the store. And that's one of the many reasons all of us love our new mother: she's a good egg!

♡

Thirteen Pounds Fills an Empty Nest

By Jean Fogle

W hen you're raising children, it's easy to lose track of time. When you're busy dealing with diapers, temper tantrums, and toddlers, the years roll by. The challenge of teenagers, especially dating and driving, soon replace the toddler years.

Before I knew it—and frankly before I was ready—our oldest son was preparing to leave for college. A few weeks before Kevin's departure, my husband, Terry, anticipating my loneliness, surprised me with an eight-week-old puppy named Molly.

After years of having my help shunned, I once again had something that actually needed me! Suddenly, I was thrown back into the toddler days. Mopping up her few accidents brought back memories and made me appreciate the ease of potty training a puppy compared to a toddler. When the boys were babies, I found myself very fond of baby talk. Once the boys reached a certain age, baby talk wasn't allowed anymore. John, at two years, expressed his displeasure: "Momma, I no baby!" and would furiously scowl if I slipped into my beloved baby babble.

Molly had no such qualms; in fact, her tail wagged even harder when I used that high baby voice. Unable to voice her opinion, she good-naturedly continued to let me indulge. Cocking her head, she understood all of the names we invented for her, including a few really obscure names, such as Quikie and Pookabrooni. The easy affection of my toddlers was remembered in the slurpy kisses of a puppy. She never rejected my hugs and attention as growing children do. Forging ahead of me on our walks didn't signal her embarrassment to be seen with me, just her enthusiasm for life.

When the boys were young, they were always eager to take day trips. As they got older, they had better things to do than spend the day with their mom. Any trip that involved a detour was greeted by a loud chorus of groans and sighs. But now I had a traveling companion that was as eager to travel as I was. The minute the car door opened, a terrier appeared in the passenger seat, ready to ride shotgun. Any stop along the way was cause for excitement, with enticing smells and the possibility of begging food from complete strangers.

When Kevin left for college, it wasn't as traumatic as I thought it would be. It was hard to focus on being lonely when a tiny terrier wanted to play or go for a walk. As I spent a good part of my days keeping her out of trouble, I realized that I was neglecting my freelance photography business. When I resumed taking pictures, the slides I got back no longer featured my primary topic, gardens. On each roll of slides there were pictures of Molly sleeping, Molly with a ball, Molly being chased by the cats, and even Molly begging. She was so cute; I found it impossible not to take pictures of her.

Molly's circle of friends widened when I took her to obedience classes, and her friends' pictures started showing up in my photo files. I discovered that taking pictures of dogs was a lot more fun than photographing gardens. It is often said that when one door closes, a new one opens. I realized that Molly had not only helped ease the transition of Kevin leaving for college but she had led me down a new path in life. Her smiling face and wagging tail has charmed people into telling me about their dogs, often leading to stories to write about or photos to take. As my focus switched from garden writing to dog writing, my husband encouraged me to quit my day job and write full-time.

Next, our youngest son, John, left for college. When I shed a few tears, Molly didn't sit on my lap and lick my face. Instead she cocked her head and looked at me before jumping off the sofa, grabbing her tennis ball, and nudging it toward me. In her dog wisdom, she knew that, for me, activity was the best cure. A few throws later, I was smiling.

I am grateful that my children were ready and able to fly the nest, and thankful that a thirteen-pound dynamo has not only filled the nest but added a new dimension to our lives. She has taught me to try new things, open my heart to new friends, take each day as it comes, and live in the moment.

Baby-Talk Mom

By Louis A. Hill Jr.

Before our sweet blond baby girl arrived, my wife—a registered nurse—decided to be a stay-at-home mother. That decision worked great for all three of us—Jeanne, me, and our little Dawn. Each evening Jeanne excitedly shared Dawn's latest accomplishment with me—when she first rolled over, her first tooth sawing through, her first word, and first step.

When Dawn was not quite two years old, our little David arrived. Jeanne and the babies were very happy, and now Jeanne was sharing each new antic of both of them with me. But by David's first birthday, my normally intelligent wife's sharing shocked and alarmed me. Jeanne now used mostly one- or two-syllable words: "Baby sits up!" and "Dawn goes bye-bye with Grandma." She was talking baby talk to me! And here's the one that I couldn't ignore: "Da-Da want more birthday cake?" Not unusual, I tried to assure myself, since she only talked to a baby and a toddler all day and seldom spoke to adults. But. . . .

Well, it was *my* turn to share this time. So I revealed my problem to Jeanne. She couldn't believe me at first. Then we had a good laugh, and I finally got the courage to suggest a remedy:

"How about using a babysitter for two days a week while you do part-time nursing?"

"Wouldn't work," she said. "Remember? I tried part-time before Dawn was born, but the hospital kept pressing me for more and more days and, feeling guilty, I was soon working four days a week. I don't want to leave Dawn and David with sitters that long."

"Then what? Think about it and let's come up with something that gets you out with adults and stimulates your thinking."

At dinner the next evening, after I'd heard all about the kids' latest antics delivered in their mom's baby talk, Jeanne said, "I've been thinking about something I might like to do that will get me away from the kids for a few hours." I looked up, more than a little excited. "Years ago, another student and I started a weekly newspaper at our nursing school," she said. "I really enjoyed writing feature articles for it, but I didn't care for the straight reporting. So maybe I would enjoy a class or two in creative writing."

The next day I rushed to check on creative writing courses offered at nearby Tulsa University's downtown division. Offered at night, the courses were taught by LaVere Anderson, then editor of the *Tulsa World's* Sunday Book Pages. Before she moved to Tulsa, she had written hundreds of short stories and articles that were published in magazines across the country, and she was still selling. When I told Jeanne, she was excited and especially happy that the courses were offered at night because I could stay with the kids while she was gone.

Though Jeanne went to class only two nights a week, her class was filled with bright people, and her teacher was superb. Not only did Jeanne's baby talk disappear, but I soon had my interesting conversationalist across the breakfast table from me. If that's all that those writing classes had accomplished, it would have been enough.

But it wasn't. There was more benefit to come: two years after her first class, Jeanne sold her first article, and three weeks after that, she sold her first short story. The years of writing that followed never encroached upon her mothering because she wrote while the children napped in the afternoon (or later when they were at school). In fact, the mothering helped her writing because her first articles were sold to mother and baby magazines. In time she developed her niche—writing narrative-style articles, each building to a gem of truth at the end. Some of those, called "Art of Living" articles, sold and were published by *Reader's Digest*.

Shortly after our third child was born, she started writing a monthly column called TLC (Tender Loving Care) for the newsstand magazine *Children's Playmate*. By the time that child, Dixon, started kindergarten, Jeanne's published stories were being chosen for anthologies, and Word Books had just published her first book while she was writing another for Judson Press.

An inspirational writer and speaker, my wife is now a contributing editor to *Guideposts* magazine. She always enjoyed being a "room mother" at our children's schools and teaching Sunday school classes as well. But what she considers her greatest accomplishment is being a happy stay-at-home mom for our three children. And I am happy to have had a small part in pointing a baby-talking mom toward a career as a successful, professional writer who has been my wonderful wife and best friend for fifty-seven years.

With Mom's Love

By Judy L. Adourian

T o this day I don't know how I remembered the correct numbers or how I kept myself from shaking long enough to dial them. I don't remember the exact words I spoke to my mother or the responses she gave. What I do remember were the conflicting emotions of guilt and relief when I heard my mother answer my 4:00 AM phone call. I distinctly remember the way she dropped everything, drove the hour and a half to my house, and hugged me as I sobbed uncontrollably in her arms. And although I didn't believe it at the time, I remember her saying, "Everything will be okay."

For the first month after birthing my second child, I assumed my inability to sleep was caused by normal natal interruptions to my usual sleeping habits. By the second month, when my newborn slept from midnight to six, I worried about why my brain wouldn't turn off long enough for me to fall asleep, too. Constantly I paced my house well into the night, unable to sit still much less lie down and envious of my husband and two sons dozing peacefully. My stomach ached with constant pain, like a deep, bottomless pit. Without warning I would burst into tears, sobs gushing forth as though a loved one had died, while in my head I kept telling myself to get a grip. I hated seeing my husband drive to work each morning. I feared that I couldn't handle both children and that my incessant, irrepressible crying would psychologically scar my boys for life. For two months I forced myself to put up a brave front for my family, but when exhaustion overtook me, my mother rescued me.

Only a woman who had lived through such anguish could recognize and vocalize the physical, mental, and emotional pain that eluded my own vocabulary. Mom explained the reality of the situation to my husband, and as he took over full responsibility for the kids, Mom took charge of nursing me back to health. She called my midwife and got an immediate appointment. She acted as my voice to tell the midwife what I couldn't verbalize, and as my brain to choose the best recovery plan. Mom worked with the midwife to enroll me in a weeklong outpatient therapy program at the hospital. She made sure that I filled my antidepressant and antianxiety prescriptions—and that I took them. Mom took me to my chiropractor, filled him in on my situation, lined up more frequent appointments, and brought me to them. And when guilt engulfed my heart at not being able to give my older son the third birthday party he deserved, my mother comforted me by saying, "You are working hard to give him back his mother. That's the greatest gift you could ever give him."

As I improved, Mom backed off, always careful to be a loving and welcome help in my life and that of my family's without ever becoming an intrusion. And whenever I stumbled, like when I thought I didn't need my medication anymore, Mom returned with her helping hands and loving heart. She never chided or berated me for being stubborn, just gently guided me back onto the right path.

To this day, I do not know how my mother survived her own horror of postpartum depression without aid from her own mother. I also cannot comprehend how she could bear to cope with the painful emotions that resurfaced for her while she selflessly helped me. What I do know is that, through the pain we each endured thirty-one years apart, we now share a sacred bond that bestows upon us the deepest level of respect, admiration, and love. What I know without a doubt is that with Mom's love, everything will be okay.

When You Least Expect It

By Maria Bailey

Country music legend Garth Brooks sings a song in which the lyrics best capture the emotions of our adoptions. The song is titled "Unanswered Prayers," and for those who prefer other music genres, the lyrics go something like this, "sometimes some of God's greatest gifts are unanswered prayers." Every time I listen to this song, it brings back the moments of desperation when motherhood seemed unobtainable, when a boycott of weekly Mass seemed like the right response to God's injustice, and the jubilation we felt each time we added another child to our family.

My journey into motherhood began well before my wedding as I prepared my body with prenatal vitamins and a regular routine of exercise. My husband Tim and I intended to have a large family, and we wanted to begin as soon as we sealed the deal with a few "I do's." Two years later we realized that a greater power was at work. Fortunately, my gynecologist also specialized in infertility, and we shared a friendship that provided her with an understanding of my deep commitment to becoming a mother.

We began all the testing, prodding, poking, needle stabbing, sperm spinning, and frustration that goes with infertility treatments. After a year of failed attempts to conceive, my husband and I decided to answer the most important question any wannabe parents should ask themselves: "What is the reason for wanting a child in your life: is it to create genic lineage or to parent a child?" We quickly realized that our goal was to create a family in whatever manner it defined itself. We wanted to be parents rather than the keepers of our gene pool. It became clear one night that my definition of motherhood went far beyond the gene pool we possessed.

We made the conscious decision to finish the cycle of infertility we had started that month and then filed papers to adopt a baby. After all, that's what it was all about—a baby. Because of my husband's age, we were unable to be considered by several adoption agencies such as Children's Home Society. We decided that a private adoption attorney would be the best option. After interviewing several attorneys, we moved forward with filling out paperwork and "getting our names on the list of prospective parents."

Good fortune came when we got a call that we had been matched with a birthmother only three weeks later. Our baby was to be born in September. Finally, we would be parents. I completed my last round of infertility the week that we met our young birthmother. She was only sixteen but healthy and seemingly prepared to give her baby up for adoption. We had a successful visit with her and then happily left on what we planned to be our last adult-only vacation.

Upon our return home from a relaxing trip together, I received a phone call that our birthmother had changed her mind. Her friends told her that if she kept her baby, she would be eligible for a number of government subsidies. The baby we had emotionally and mentally bonded with would not be coming to us in September. It was a Friday, so I spent all weekend on the couch, lifeless except for the whimper of tears that streamed endlessly down my cheeks. It took every bit of energy to finally leave the couch on Monday for a previously scheduled doctor's appointment. As I sadly entered my gynecologist's office to give yet another ounce of blood, the entire staff could read the bad news on my face. I am not even sure I felt Roz, the nurse, draw blood from my arm. My head hung down and I stared at the tiled floor as Roz performed her routine lab tests on my blood.

To this day, I still remember the pattern of the floor tiles and Roz's feet as they left the ground. Her screams of delight totally took me off guard as she proclaimed to every human being within a five-mile radius that I was pregnant. It was a moment I will *never* forget. My feeling of sadness at our failed adoption quickly turned to exhilaration over our pregnancy. That night we celebrated as I announced our success to my husband. Little did I know that the next morning would bring even greater joy into our lives.

The next morning, our adoption attorney called to tell us that we were matched with a new birthmother and the baby was due the same week as the first baby. My husband and I decided that this was the plan we had not been privy to and we would move forward with the adoption and with our pregnancy. Our two babies would be born within six months of each other. We also decided not to tell any of our family or friends about the first failed attempt at adoption to eliminate the need for them to worry.

Our birthmother was an unwed teenager who already had another child. The thought of raising two babies was overwhelming for her. She had decided that she wanted her baby to have Catholic parents, thus choosing us from among others. Shortly after the selection process, we met her for dinner, along with her boyfriend, who was also the birthfather. She also brought her two-year-old daughter who would be the half sister of our child. The meeting went well. We had decided to keep our identity protected so we only used first names. The time together was spent sharing stories, family histories, and getting to know each other. We gave our birthmother a beeper number to call should she want to talk with me. The beeper number allowed her to contact us without the knowledge of our phone number or area code. She was open to sharing her doctor visits with me and eventually invited me to attend a few with her. We paid for her health care and living expenses during her pregnancy.

It was a very strange experience to watch the growth of two babies in two different wombs at the same time. As our birthmother proceeded through her pregnancy, I proceeded through mine. We were advised to keep our pregnancy a secret from our birthmother to prevent any second thoughts on her behalf. According to our attorney, many young women desire to give their babies to families who "cannot have one of their own." Fortunately, Mother Nature was kind to me and I gained very little weight during the first four months of pregnancy.

One of the greatest gifts our birthmother gave me was the

ability to be in the delivery room with her at the time of my daughter's birth. It was one of the most amazing experiences I've ever witnessed to see my daughter emerge into the world. I watched as our birthmother suffered through labor without any drugs, pushed with all her might, and finally delivered a beautiful baby girl. I will never forget the moment she turned to me and said, "Now you have your family." Every nurse in the room had tears in their eyes.

Happily, we welcomed Madison Bailey, our first daughter, into our family and five months later gave her a brother, Owen Bailey, when I gave birth. Just fifteen months after a month of infertility drugs, we added another son, Keena, to our rapidly growing family. What started as a journey that seemed to be leading to a childless future quickly turned into a very busy household with three babies under twenty months. My prayers had seemingly gone unanswered for many months but in the end were instead answered with abundance.

Most parents would feel content with three wonderful babies, except for those who had more than fifteen siblings between them. When Tim and I decided to try for a fourth baby, no one was really surprised. We loved the chaos of children, so we began fertility drugs again when the youngest of the three turned four. Again, I prayed for success that failed to happen. A freak infection caused by a botched insemination landed me in the hospital. As I lay in a hospital bed, my best girlfriend asked me if the fourth baby had to come from my womb. The question provoked me to consider adoption again, and then fate stepped into the process. My obstetrician decided she was going to take me to dinner in her new Porsche when I got out of the hospital, but she had a wreck on the way to my house and broke her hands. The injury was severe enough to force her to close down her practice. I take pride in learning lessons once, so I knew God had plans other than a pregnancy for me. A few days later I ran into my adoption attorney and told her the story of my recent attempt to get pregnant. I mentioned to her that we were interested in adopting again. She informed me that it was rare for a birthmother to give her child to a big family like ours, but she would keep me in mind.

Less than two months later, I got a call from our adoption attorney. She recounted a story about a girl who had come into her office this particular day. She apparently resembled me, and my attorney told her the story of our adoption, birth, and desire to adopt again in jest because she thought we were crazy wanting four children under four years of age. The meeting went on without any further mention of us, and the reason for the call was only to tell me how much this young birthmother looked like me. However, the conversation changed that evening when the attorney phoned me at home with good news. The birthmother had called her back and asked if the crazy woman she had heard about would adopt her child. She liked the idea of her baby living in a big family. We, of course, said yes and thus our family grew through the adoption of our second daughter only four months later.

The adoption process went virtually the same as the first. I shared doctor appointments with our birthmother, though I was not invited to be in the delivery room. The one element that was different with our second adoption was the amount of information I collected from our birthmother. She expressed fear that the baby would not know her when she was older. I assured her that I would tell her stories of her biological mother, and to reconfirm my commitment to this, I gave her a baby book to fill out. She filled out all the prenatal and family history and gave it to me. I promised I would complete the postbirth information and give it to our daughter in her teen years. I feel very fortunate to have so much information to share with her later.

Four years and three children later, after suffering through infertility and praying for a child, we were blessed with Morgan. Our prayers had indeed been answered in a different manner than I had ever anticipated.

In the end, the greatest gift was the fact that my prayers had not been answered when I asked God for a baby. For if God had given me a baby when I had asked, I would never have adopted my beautiful daughters. And today I could not imagine my life without them in it. Sometimes God's greatest gifts are indeed unanswered prayers.

♡

The Wind
Beneath Our
Wings

Wordplay

By D. B. Zane

"**M**om, do we have any poster board?" I asked one Saturday afternoon.

She scrounged around the garage. "Here we go. I think this side is good enough." One side had footprints all over it. The other was nearly all white.

"It's perfect," I said. I knew that I could cover the few dirt spots and no one would know.

"Need any help?"

"Nope." I returned to my room and set to work. Miss Taylor, my English teacher, had given us an assignment. As I search my memory today, I cannot really remember it—something about playing with words. And I had hit upon the perfect idea. Surely this would raise my English grade.

I was not the best artist in the world. Shoot, I couldn't even draw a straight line. Still, for being in seventh grade, I thought I was doing great. I drew connected squares all around the poster to be the path for my word game.

"Honey, you've been in there for hours," Mom said as she came into the room. "What are you making?"

"A word game," I replied proudly. "I'm just about finished with the board."

Mom inspected it. "Looks wonderful. I like all those colors."

"Now for the cards." I looked around my messy desk. "Do we have any index cards?"

After I gave up searching my room and Mom had no luck in her desk, she returned to find some—in mine. They were kind of big and I was running out of time.

"You write; I'll cut," Mom offered, and she cut them all into perfect little squares.

I already had my list of questions. They were plays on words, things having to do with homonyms or words with more than one meaning. Sometime before the project, Miss Taylor had given us a list. I made sure I used every one of those words and racked my brain to add some of my own. I even appealed to my family over dinner and spent the meal taking notes as we all laughed and got pretty silly. Still, I did get some good ideas.

My brother hoped the ideas wouldn't raze my grade—another wordplay.

Finally, the day arrived. I'd never been so excited that it was Monday. Mom had found the perfect box—okay, it wasn't like the ones you get in the store when you buy a board game, but it was good enough for me.

As I waited for class to begin, actually glad that I had English first period, I had visions of Miss Taylor being so impressed that she canceled her lesson plan for that day and allowed the class to play the game. No one else in the class had thought of it. It was my idea alone. Surely an A+ was in my future.

When we turned in our work, Miss Taylor gave no hint at all that she was impressed. Then again, she never smiled. Plus, it was just a box. She was going to have to actually open it and play the game.

It took her forever, and I mean forever, to grade this project. Finally, on Friday, she returned them with our grades. Attached to my box was a sheet of paper with my name on it. In red ink, she had written a gigantic "F+"!

F+! F+? Surely there was some mistake. I wanted to storm up to her and demand justice. My legs were jelly. I just sat there, trying not to cry.

I don't remember the rest of the day. All I remember was a giant red F+ emblazoned on my brain. The tears came pouring out when I arrived home. Mom's shirt was soaked by the time I started calming down. Through it all, Mom just held me, rocking me gently. Then, when she decided I was ready, she asked, "What happened?"

I opened my mouth to answer and felt the tears forming again. Instead, I pulled out that horrid piece of paper and began to unfold it. "My word game." I choked out. She looked at the paper and was quiet for a moment.

"F plus," she said quietly. "F plus."

I'd have gotten mad at her for repeating it, for even saying it out loud, but there was something in her tone that made me curious. I looked up at her expectantly.

"Well, I was just thinking . . . what does the plus mean?" she asked.

"What?"

"I mean, does it say that it's higher than an F? Is that better or worse? What exactly is extra 'effy'?"

"Extra 'effy'? F plus. Better than an F." It was kind of ridiculous. "Either it's an F or not."

I smiled for the first time all day. That plus was pretty stupid. And for a brief moment, I forgot all about what that red F meant. Leave it to my mom to make me feel better by finding the humor in it.

"Come on. After dinner, the whole family will play your game. F plus. Extra fabulous, fantastic, phenomenal, first-rate fun."

Mom Saved the Day

By Georgia A. Hubley

It was the day before school was out for the summer, and during the bus ride home from school, several classmates talked about the parting gifts they'd be giving our fifth grade teacher, Mrs. Counter, the following day. I didn't join in the conversation, as I was ashamed my family couldn't afford such a gift.

How I wished my family were rich. Then I felt a tinge of guilt as I thought about the night before, when my folks assumed I was sound asleep and I overheard their conversation about money being scarce. Even though the spring corn crop had been planted and was thriving, there'd be no extra money until the corn was harvested in the fall.

When I arrived home from school, Mom greeted me at the door, "Only one more day to go!" she exclaimed.

My eyes welled up with tears, "I don't want to go to school tomorrow. I don't have a gift for my teacher," I wailed.

Mom stroked my hair and dried my tears with her apron, "You are very artistic and can make her a nice handmade farewell card with the assortment of craft paper in your desk," she said. "I'll help. Come with me."

I followed Mom to her flower garden, and we gathered pink moss rose petals, various seedpods, and shiny green leaves for the card. That afternoon, we sat at the picnic table on the back porch, cut, pasted, and created a pretty card. We left the card on the picnic table to dry overnight.

I woke up early the next morning, my excitement growing as I thought of the summer months ahead and no school until fall. I dressed quickly and ran downstairs. After breakfast, I went outside to get the card.

As I approached the picnic table, my breath caught in my throat—only a pile of shredded leaves and purple craft paper remained. "Mom, come quick, my card is ruined! It's been chewed into hundreds of pieces!" I shouted, tears streaming down my cheeks.

"It looks like the field mice I spotted yesterday in our vegetable garden helped themselves to a snack. They thought you made the card for them," Mom said. Mom's explanation only made me cry harder. In between sobs, I cried out, "What can I do? There's not enough time to make another card."

"Oh, don't fret," Mom said. "If we hurry, we can pick a few flowers and make a corsage for your teacher."

As Mom quickly broke off a spray of clusters of small white flowers from a spirea bush, she instructed me to break off three small branches of bright pink, bell-shaped flowers from a nearby weigela bush. When finished, we scurried to the back porch and spread the flowers across the picnic table; then, with garden shears, Mom snipped off even sections from the branches of the flowers we'd gathered. I watched in awe as she intertwined the branches of flowers, alternated the colors to form a corsage, and gently tied the flowers together with green thread. For a final touch she added a shiny white bow, and then handed me the corsage. "Hon, you better scoot. You don't want to miss the bus."

"It's so beautiful. Thank you, thank you," I said, as I kissed her cheek.

When I arrived at school, I went directly to my classroom and placed the corsage among the other gifts on Mrs. Counter's desk. Afterward, a classmate taunted, "Flowers aren't a gift." Giggles ensued. A wave of embarrassment washed over me. Mrs. Counter glared at the class, then reached for the corsage. "What lovely flowers. Thank you for the wonderful gift," she said, smiling broadly at me. Suddenly, the room was quiet, as everyone watched her pin on the corsage.

"You're welcome," I replied, beaming proudly. "I helped my mom make it."

"Please thank your mother for me," she said. "You are both very creative."

I was glad all classes were dismissed at noon on the last day of school. All morning, I'd barely been able to contain my exuberance, as I wanted to tell Mom how much Mrs. Counter liked the corsage.

The bus ride home from school that afternoon seemed longer than usual. When the school bus finally stopped at the lane leading to our farmhouse, I leaped down the steps and ran all the way home. When I met Mom on the front porch, I was out of breath and gulped for air. "Mrs. Counter loved the corsage and she said we are both very creative," I said.

Mom grinned. "I'm glad she liked the gift. Since there are so many gorgeous flowers in bloom, let's make more corsages and give them to all the neighbors."

We began making corsages that very afternoon. Patiently, Mom taught me how to assemble the flowers. It wasn't long until I could make corsages all by myself. Like Mom, I, too, added my own artistic flair to each corsage. "I love flowers, especially roses!" I exclaimed.

"Does that mean you'll stop grumbling when I ask you to help weed the flower beds?" Mom teased.

I giggled and replied, "Maybe."

Years have passed since I was ten and Mom saved the day. I am grown now and have a creative family of my own. I will be forever grateful to Mom for giving me free reign to indulge my creativity, my imagination, and my dreams from childhood to adulthood.

A Mother's Miracle

By Michael Jordan Segal

That unforgettable day was February 18, 1981. My girl-friend, Sharon, had to return to her college dormitory in the wee hours of the morning after studying with me in the library at the University of Texas in Austin. She told me that she had to return for a good night's sleep because she had an exam the next morning. Also, being somewhat tired myself, I agreed, and we got into my car, not realizing that our lives would soon be changed forever.

I noticed the gas gauge was almost on empty, so I quickly turned into an all-night convenience store to purchase some gaso-line. I noticed my wallet was empty, so I borrowed two dollars from Sharon and shouted, "I'll be right back to pump the gas as soon as I pay the attendant inside." I ran toward the store, not realizing what was behind the shaded glass doors.

Unfortunately for me, the store was in the midst of a robbery. One of the thieves forced me into the cooler, shoved me down, and pumped a .38 caliber shell into the back of my head. He thought I was dead, as did many others in the ensuing hours. However, there was still a faint pulse in my body.

At the hospital, the entire staff was pessimistic. The neurosurgeon went home just after I was brought to the hospital, as he was sure I would be dead by morning. My mother, when she arrived at the hospital, overheard a nurse speaking about me: "Even if he survives, he'll be a *vegetable*." (Maybe that is why I still do not like vegetables.) But my mother never wavered in her faith. She was determined to get me better, no matter what anyone said or felt.

When the neurosurgeon returned in the morning, he was quite surprised to see me still alive. He greeted my parents with his plans: "It's difficult to believe that he's still alive. However, it's now mandatory to operate in order to reduce the pressure on his brain. Your son has a 60 percent chance of dying on the operating room table before the end of the three-and-a-half-hour surgery." With those words my mother automatically thought, "Great—that means that Mike has a 40 percent chance of living."

The doctor quickly continued, "But even if he beats the odds and makes it through the surgery, he will probably never communicate with anyone, never function normally, never recognize the two of you, never know an 'a' from a 'b' from a 'c' . . . ." My mother could not endure the intensity of the doctor's negativity. This was her "precious Michael" that he was talking about, so she blotted all of the statements out of her mind. While my mother dealt with these facts with denial, my father quickly became extremely depressed.

The doctor concluded his remarks and left the conference room to perform, probably in his mind, a futile operation, but I was still alive at the end of the surgery. The neurosurgeon came out after the operation, still quite negative as he discussed my condition. As he left, my mother quickly and optimistically stated to my father, "Now we need to rent a mini-warehouse to keep Mike's belongings in for when he returns to school."

My father stood there in shock—first, at what had happened to me, and second, at my mother's unrealistic statement. "Toby, didn't you hear what the doctor said?" my father angrily asked. "He explained that our son would be lucky to make it to a nursing home."

My mother snapped back, "Look, Mike's doctor may be an eminent neurosurgeon, *but he doesn't know my son!* Now, can we look for that warehouse?"

My father passively went with my mother to look for the mini-warehouse, one that he thought would never be opened by me. My mother truly believed that I would eventually return to the university.

Shortly after that time, I began to show some very slight signs of progress. Countless people prayed for me, but one very persistent and very determined mother prayed for a miracle for her son.

After three long weeks that felt like an emotional roller coaster for my family, the neurosurgeon told my parents that I was stable enough to be flown to a rehabilitation hospital in Houston, my hometown. My mother was elated with the news. I had been in a coma and then in a stupor. True, I was still unable to walk or talk, but now, *I was going home!*

Even though in Houston I was continuing to make small progress, that progress was not consistent enough for many. However, my mother never gave up her hope or faith in me.

Then, one eventful morning, I was tested by the hospital neuropsychologist, who stated after my tests, "Mike, I know you have dreams of returning to college. However, judging from the tests I just gave, you will never be able to return to college. You will be happier if you focus on more realistic goals."

I was devastated, as I believed I was making great strides. I was furious with the neuropsychologist, as I thought, "Who are you to tell me what I can or cannot do?" I had made a goal for myself to one day, somehow, return to the University of Texas. I still had a long way to go; I still had to relearn to do so many things that the vast majority of people simply took for granted.

When my mother came to the hospital that day, she could tell that something was wrong. Even though I could barely speak, by asking me a series of yes and no questions my "meek" mother discovered what was bothering me. She stormed out of my room and pounded on the neuropsychologist's office door. When the neuropsychologist answered, she stated, "Mrs. Segal, you're interrupting my patient."

"*How dare you!*" my mother boomed. She continued, "I know you upset Mike. I don't want you to ever talk to him again! My husband and I believe in accentuating the positive and eliminating the negative, but you seem driven on emphasizing the negative with Michael and ignoring the positive. *Leave him alone!*"

It was as if my mother had had a judge issue a restraining order. I guess the proverb is true: "Don't mess with a mother." I am not sure how my mother "moved" me to increase my progress, but shortly after my experience with the neuropsychologist, my right leg began to move slightly, followed the next week by some movement in my right arm, followed the next week by me finally beginning to speak two words together. I was really making steady progress, and as days, weeks, and months went by, very few people could believe how much I had improved—that is, except for my mother. She knew the power of a mother's prayers.

A year and a half after almost losing my life at the convenience store near the University of Texas, I returned to Austin to reopen that mini-warehouse that stored my belongings so that I could continue my college education. Four years after that day, I graduated at the top of my class, due in large part to my mother, the woman who showed me that sometimes miracles do happen. She showed me the importance of persistence. I still have limitations because of the shooting; however, my mother drilled into me the concept of "never giving up" because God does answer prayers.

For all that she taught me, I can only repay her in a very small way: Mom, I love you!

Follow Your Heart

By Sallie A. Rodman

"You're what?" my husband, Paul, yelled into the phone. "Well, we're coming down there to take you to dinner tomorrow night. You've got some explaining to do and it better be good."

"What was that all about?" I asked.

"Seems our son is flunking out of college," he replied angrily.

"That's impossible," I replied, "he's one of the smartest kids around."

"I don't get it either, but we'll get to the bottom of this."

The next morning my husband had an emergency sales call and couldn't make it back in time for the dinner.

"Not to worry; I'll handle it. They don't call me Mom for nothing," I smiled.

With Pat's hectic class schedule, we had started weekly phone chats, so I felt one of our "heart-to-hearts" might be a better approach. I caught up with him at his dorm the next afternoon.

"Pat, this is Mom talking here," I said in a conciliatory tone. "Let's cut to the chase. What's up with your grades?"

"Oh, I don't know. Well . . . actually, I hate my business classes," Pat said. "I just can't get excited about them."

"What do you mean, you can't get excited about them? If you don't like business, what are you doing as a business major?"

"Well, everyone says you make a lot of money in business."

"Pat, it's not strictly about making money," I replied. "Honey, you have to love what you do. You have to be excited and passionate about your career. If you don't love it, embrace it, no amount of money will make you happy. Besides, you have certain talents and you need to use them. Isn't there something that turns you on?"

"There is," he replied. "I love fooling around with music and sound. Not singing or playing an instrument but dubbing and mixing the sound. We have a new recording studio on campus, and when I get in there, it is so cool."

"Don't they have a major for that?" I asked.

"I think there is a new one called 'Recording Arts,' but I already have so many business units. I don't want to start over."

"Well, check it out, Pat. You're going to be working for a long time; it better be something you love. You have to follow your heart. Take it from your ol' mom here."

That conversation stands out in my memory, and I will cherish it forever.

Pat did change majors and graduated with honors as one of the first recording arts majors at Loyola. He got to use all his business credits for a minor in business.

Unfortunately, he could not do an internship his senior year because he had to work on campus to help pay his tuition. So he had to pay his dues. He got a job as a "gofer" with a postproduction studio after graduation. He cleaned up after rock bands, ran out to get hamburgers for the crew, and sometimes got to try his hand at the sound recording equipment. Times were tough, and Pat gradually became worn down by barely making minimum wage. He seldom paid his rent on time, had little money for groceries, and showed up at home for at least one square meal a week. He started living off his credit cards, and pretty soon he was head over heels in debt.

Pat's faith was at an all-time low, and I have to admit it was getting harder for me to encourage him to follow his dream. I worried a lot about our son during that time and hoped I had given him the right advice.

Meanwhile, Pat was bone weary and decided to take fate into his own hands. He quit his job at the studio and used his minor in business to start working at a large rental car company. Within six months he was setting all sales records and within a year became district manager. There was no stopping his boundless energy. He was making great money, paying off his debts, and was generally happy, or so we thought. One night Pat called.

"Mom, we gotta talk." I held my breath. His voice sounded hollow and forlorn.

"What's up, kiddo?"

"I can't do it anymore. I've been holding it in, but I can't pretend anymore. I feel like something is missing in my life." I expected him to say a girlfriend or wife. He'd been working long hours with no time to date.

"It's my job, Mom. Remember how you used to tell me to do

what I love? Well, I hate what I'm doing. Oh, sure, the money is great, but I'm miserable."

"Pat, why don't you give your dream one more try? If it's meant to be, it will happen," I counseled. My heart went out to my only son whom I loved so much.

So Pat set out with renewed faith, and I prayed he would succeed. Well, it seems a friend of a friend knew someone who worked at a studio, and they happened to need an assistant. Pat was hired, and late at night when everyone had left, he got hands-on experience. First he became an assistant engineer, then graduated to sound engineer. He kept right on learning, and I kept right on praying.

One day the phone rang and I could hardly make out the excited chatter on the other end of the line.

"Mom, hang on to your hat . . . you won't believe it . . . I am so excited . . . now don't get too blown away—are you sitting down?"

"Enough!" I yelled. "What is it?"

"I've been, I mean, we've been, well, the whole sound crew has been nominated for an Emmy."

"Oh, Pat!" I screamed. Tears filled my eyes. He had done it. I don't think there was a prouder mom in all creation that day.

As for the money, well, you'll have to ask Pat about that. You can find him working long hours at his own recording studio when he isn't home with his new wife.

To Keep Me from the Rain

By Joyce Stark

Sometimes it's not the huge sacrifices that moms make, or even the countless things they do day in and day out that make you realize what really special people they are.

It was just a typical dull and windy January day here in the northeast of Scotland. When I left home for the office where I worked in Arbroath, the next town, the weather forecasters said, "Windy and cold, but no rain." Naturally, by the time I was about to leave work in the early evening, it was absolutely pouring!

My office was close to the bus stop, so that was no problem; I just shot out the door and on to the bus. Unfortunately, once I got home to Montrose, I had about a mile to walk from the bus stop to my home. Normally on a night like this, if my husband was home, he would get into the car and come and get me. That morning he had told me that he was putting the car in for service and that it would be in overnight. With my total faith in the weather forecasters, I slipped my small folding umbrella into my handbag before I set off.

As I stepped off the bus that night to walk home, I struggled to get my tiny umbrella to go up in the strong wind. It had a sunny pattern on it and was obviously designed for a very light shower somewhere on the Mediterranean, not a Scottish downpour! To my amazement, I heard my mom's voice say, "Quickly, come under here before you get soaked!"

I nipped under the bigger umbrella and stared at Mom in surprise. "What on earth are you doing here in this weather?" I asked her. My mom was eighty-three that year, and although fit and healthy, she didn't normally like going out in strong wind and heavy rain. In fact, if we got a few days like that, I usually nipped round to her house to make sure she didn't run out of anything.

"You said to come round for tea tonight, but I came early before the rain got too heavy. Eric told me that your car was in for servicing, and I saw your umbrella lying on the chair. I guessed that you had set it out to take with you but had forgotten it. Eric was on the telephone, so I just picked it up and came out so that I could meet you and you wouldn't get soaked!"

That happened a number of years ago, and my mom passed away the following year. It's the incident that sticks most strongly in my mind and just sums up how completely my mom loved me. She wouldn't have gone out in the wind and rain for herself, but she never gave a second thought about it because I, who was so much younger and fitter, might get wet on my way home!

I just stopped and gave her a hug, and as the umbrella shook all over the place and we both got a little wet, she asked in surprise, "What on earth was that for?"

Only she could possibly have asked me that!

The Banished-to-Bed Birthday

By Annmarie B. Tait

Easter Sunday fell on April 21 in 1957, and a special Easter it was, for that was the day I was born. Everything went swimmingly as far as birthday galas were concerned until 1964 when I turned seven. Oh, how I looked forward to that birthday! It was no secret that second grade was one hot spot of activity on birthdays. I'd made it all the way from September to April watching one birthday bash after another, and tomorrow it was going to be my turn at bat.

Birthday girls and boys had every privilege known to mankind in the second grade universe. They got to open the windows in the morning with the window pole, lead the "Pledge of Allegiance," and be the only one to say "God Bless America" at the end. As if that wasn't enough, they passed out cupcakes to their classmates smack-dab in the middle of the afternoon and picked the daily song we sang just before the close of the day. To top the whole thing off, the birthday student had no homework on that day. I ask you, could a second grader want for any more than that?

And it was all just sitting on the edge of my plate waiting to roll right into the center when I noticed a funny rash on my belly that night after my bath. "Look at this, Mommy, my stomach has polka dots." I heard the faint sound of my mother's voice muttering "Uh-oh," as she came down the hallway toward me to investigate the situation. I am the youngest of five children, so when my mother said, "You're not going to be happy about this, but I'm pretty sure you have the measles," even at six (almost seven, don't forget), I knew there was a lot of experience behind that statement. I also knew that the prospects of being the heralded birthday student dimmed with each new spot that appeared.

"Are you sure, Mommy? Really, really, *really* sure?"

"Well," she said, "I'm about as sure as I can be, but by tomorrow morning we'll know for certain."

Morning came and the spots had spread to my arms and cheeks, and by then I was running a fever. The shadow of doubt disappeared for good. My mother called the doctor, who stopped at our house on the way in to his office, which was just two blocks up the street. I opened my mouth and said "ahhh" while he pressed my tongue down with a big, fat Popsicle stick. Then he looked into my eyes with a flashlight that looked more like a fountain pen, and, last of all, he took a good, long look at all the spots. "It's measles all right." Case closed. Good-bye birthday bash.

After the doctor left, my mother set me up on the couch with a comfy pillow and a cozy blanket. She gave me baby aspirin and— of all things—a pair of sunglasses to wear. For whatever reason, in those days daylight was supposed to be very damaging to your eyes when you had the measles. Well, the sunglasses were fun for about ten minutes; then the movie star effect wore off and the grim disappointment of missing my birthday at school settled in.

I really didn't spend a lot of time crying and moaning over the whole thing. I was too sick for all of that. But in between my bouts of having the chills and taking naps, all I could think of was the fun I was missing at school, and no amount of toast Mommy cut into the shape of a heart to eat with my tea was going to make up for it.

After the morning cartoons were over, I went back up to my bed and slept some more. Mommy would come in and check on me every hour or so, but I was not very interested in her happy talk or her famous chicken soup, even when it arrived with a paper party hat on the tray. Mostly, I was interested in making the clear point that my birthday was ruined. I was doing a bang-up job of it, too.

Late in the afternoon as I pondered the distribution of my birthday cupcakes at school (which Mom sent along with my sister to prevent disappointed classmates), a deliciously sweet aroma floated up the steps and filled my bedroom. It was getting a lot tougher to put on a good pout with the smell of one of my mother's cakes throwing a monkey wrench into the whole plan. Laughing gas couldn't have had a stronger effect on me. So I took another nap, but this time with a smile on my face.

My brother and sisters came home from school, finished their chores and homework, and ate dinner. I was pretty much resigned to having my seventh birthday go down in the history books as the worst birthday ever. Just about then, Mommy and Daddy came marching into my bedroom with my brother and sisters in tow, and Mommy held the most amazing carousel cake I had ever seen—and she made it all by herself. It was a chocolate cake with white frosting, and red and white drinking straws sprang from the top to support the bright red cone-shaped dome that she had made out of construction paper. There were little red plastic carousel horses, and each one sported a white birthday candle sticking up right out of the saddle. It had loops of red frosting decorating the sides and a little flag attached to a toothpick sticking out of the top of the carousel that said "Happy Birthday, Annie." Everyone sang and there were presents to open, and oh, it was just a grand event. There are no two ways about it.

For years my mother joked about that cake, mostly because she was a fine baker but ran a little short in the art department. You could never convince me then, or now, that my seventh birthday cake wasn't an absolute masterpiece. After forty-four years, I still remember every detail.

♡

I'll Send You a Rainbow

By Judi Moreo

My mother married when she had just graduated from high school. She married the man of her dreams and had two beautiful little girls. She was pregnant again when her husband was killed. Two weeks later, she gave birth to twins. She now had four children, no husband, no money, and a high school education. What was she to do? She moved back home with her parents and got a job working as a seamstress in a neighbor's home business. My mom paid her mother to watch the babies, running home to see them during whatever breaks she could get. Her mother constantly encouraged her to give her four children up for adoption, since she certainly couldn't afford to keep them. My mother was adamant that she would never give up her children. She would take care of them, love them, protect them, and make a good life for them.

When the woman she worked for told her that she wasn't bringing in enough work to support them both, my mom got a job as a housekeeper at a hospital where she worked for four years. She saved what money she could and eventually was able to rent a small place of her own for her family; she hired a woman to watch the children while she worked.

Then World War II erupted, which provided women with greater opportunities for employment as men marched off to war. Daily, my mom looked in the newspaper for a better-paying job. One day she saw a classified ad for a mechanical draftsman. As my mother had always been a good artist, she applied for the job. The ad said to "bring your portfolio." She took pictures she had drawn of people, animals, and objects. The woman who interviewed her said her work was very nice, but she was looking for someone who could do technical drawings. Mother went home and sat up all night drawing pictures of nuts, bolts, and screws to scale. The next day she took them back for the interviewer to see and was hired. The company sent her to school to learn even more. She became the first mechanical draftswoman hired by that aircraft company. She went on to become a member of the design team that designed several of the aircraft used in war, and some are still in use today.

After two years, my mother married a man she had met at the hospital where she had previously worked. A year later, I was born. My mother's faith never wavered. She always believed that God was with us, loved us, protected us, and would provide what we needed when we needed it. During the following challenging years, times were tough and money was scarce, but my mom's faith was strong. She worked a full-time job, put in a garden, canned vegetables for the winter, raised chickens so we had eggs and meat, and sewed our clothing. My mom's artistic ability and her belief that you do what has to be done when it has to be done carried us through the hard times.

As I grew up, there were so many times that she sacrificed for us and so many times when she made the impossible possible. One event that has always held a special place in my heart happened when I was in high school. I was being installed as an officer in a youth organization. On the day before the installation ceremony, the advisor said we must all wear white dresses with red trim for the ceremony. A white skirt and blouse would have worked, but I didn't have either. Even if a store had been open that evening, we didn't have the money to run out and buy anything. Credit cards were nonexistent then. I was very upset.

My mother saw my frustration and asked what was wrong. When I told her that I didn't have anything to wear the next day, she said, "That is not a problem," took a sheet off the bed, got out a pattern, cut out a dress, and stayed up most of the night sewing. She trimmed it in white lace and put a red ribbon sash at the waist. She then borrowed a pair of red shoes for me from one of my older sisters. That next afternoon when the installation took place, I had the most beautiful dress at the event. That dress was the most durable dress I ever owned. I wore it for special occasions for years. It's almost impossible to wear out a sheet!

Throughout my life, whenever I had doubts about my abilities or whether or not I could do something, my mom would always say, "Draw a line. If you don't like what you've drawn, erase it and start over, but draw a line." I knew that meant that I was to have faith and believe in my ability. I had to believe and take action. Sometimes I'd cry, "But Mom, what if I do the wrong thing?" She'd say, "You'll never know if it's wrong or not unless you try." Sometimes she would quote William James, the father of modern psychology in America: "It is the faith that we have in advance of a doubtful undertaking that is what assures its successful conclusion."

When my mom was eighty-four, I moved to Africa for work. One night we were talking on the phone and laughing about my driving on the other side of the road and my adjustment to my new life. She said she was so happy for me and that she knew I had found my rightful place. Before she hung up, she said, "Whenever you get sad or lonely, remember I love you, and I'll send you a rainbow now and then to remind you." My mom passed away a few days later. I'll never know whether or not she knew that the time of her transition was imminent, but very often when I look at the sky and see a rainbow, I know she is near.

♡

Voice Above the Wind

By Marcia E. Brown

T he loud knock on the door came just after breakfast. As Mama opened the door, wind tore it from her fingers, slamming it back against the wall. Our next-door neighbor, Ruthie, stumbled in.

"Come right over, Mary! Bring your little girl to our storm cellar," Ruthie blurted out. "Hurry!"

Ruthie turned and ran, bent over against the high wind outside. It was the height of the infamous dust bowl days of the 1930s and the season for tornados. Years later this part of the Oklahoma prairie would be called Tornado Alley.

Mama looked briefly at the roiling clouds filling the sky, grabbed my hand, and we followed Ruthie. I held on as tightly to Mama as I could, scared that I might blow away as we ran. Giant tumbleweeds whipped across the yard, whirling like demons. The sky was a pressing layer of greenish-black clouds.

Most houses in our town had storm cellars, but our small frame house was not so blessed. I was four years old and would not have understood if Mama told me she was claustrophobic. Despite that fear, she did not hesitate to get us to the offered shelter. Down into Ruthie's dark cellar where we joined half a dozen neighbor women whose husbands, like my dad, had already left for work before there was a hint of danger. In those years, accurate weather forecasting was in the future and the panhandle of Oklahoma was and is known for volatile changes.

Mama appreciated Ruthie's kindness. We had not lived in the area very long, nor did we know all of our neighbors. She assumed that anyone's storm cellar would be equipped with some kind of light, water, and other necessities. Not so, we soon discovered.

Double wooden doors were set at an angle above the cellar steps. Originally planned as a fruit cellar typical of the times, in which to store home-canned foods and root vegetables, this cellar was now empty except for an old wooden table. It was simply a quick escape from a sudden storm.

Still, Mama did not worry, and in my young ignorance, neither did I. Ruthie had left one of the double doors open to let in light. Then heavy rain laced with large hail struck and the door blew shut. We found ourselves in pitch blackness, illuminated occasionally by flashes of lightning seen through cracks in the doors.

One of our companions, a recent young bride, became hysterical, crying out each time there was a crash of thunder.

Ruthie scolded, "Hush! You'll scare the child."

Mama lifted me up onto the table and stood with her arm tightly around me. I could not see her but was comforted by her hug. I was not afraid of the dark, and forty years would pass before I discovered that Mama was terrified of lightning as well as being shut in small, dark spaces.

A particularly loud clap of thunder was followed by the pistol-shot sound of lightning striking a nearby tree. Then came a crash as the tree fell across the cellar doors, trapping us inside.

By then I was beginning to feel frightened. I whimpered and was close to tears when Mama began to say nursery rhymes and to recite our favorite A. A. Milne poems from the books about Christopher Robin and Pooh, which I loved. We read those books so many times, Mama knew them by heart. Her voice was steady above the storm.

Time passed and after a while the storm moved on as quickly as it had come. As it grew quiet outside, some of the women tried to push upward on the doors so we could get out of the cellar. The doors stuck tight under the weight of the mature cottonwood tree that had fallen on it.

I could feel Mama grow tense and angry as she learned that our hospitable neighbor had not a single tool in that cellar! By then we knew, too, that no one had thought to bring matches or candles or a flashlight.

Mama began to recite other poetry. Then she sang silly songs. Except for her voice, there was no sound in the cellar, no one crying, no one hysterical again.

It seemed as if the whole day must have passed in darkness, but it was only late morning when men who lived on our block came to check on their families. Ruthie's husband saw the tree blocking the storm cellar where we waited. Finally we heard men's voices and called out. We heard a truck drive close to the cellar and men shouting as they tied the tree to the truck to haul it away. At last the doors opened and we were freed.

Mama never again went into a storm cellar. Her memories of that day were too painful. Mine were not, for what I remember most is the sweet sound of her calming voice above the wind and thunder and rain.

Years later when my sons and I were in another house on a hill in the path of another tornado, we sheltered in the safest corner, an inside hallway. Surrounded by pillows, we listened to the banshee howl of wind in a funnel cloud as it passed over the town. How puzzled and finally amused my teenagers were to hear me begin to recite familiar rhymes from their childhood and mine, my voice rising above the storm, passing on, if I could, that special gift of love and courage from my mom.

♡

The Perfect Corsage

By Connie K. Pombo

"**M**om, did you pick up Jenna's corsage?"

"No, honey, I thought you did."

"Moothhherrrrr . . . the prom is in three hours! Can you puleeeeze pick it up?"

As a mother of two sons, I've been relegated the honor of picking out and picking up corsages for my sons' dates for the last eight years. This was the final prom corsage. After nearly a decade of "prom duty," I knew the importance of details—especially corsages. But for some reason a "prom cloud" hovered over us— something *always* went wrong at the last minute

With corsage nightmares still lingering in my head, I jumped into the car and whispered a prayer: "Please let this be the 'perfect' corsage."

When I arrived at the florist shop, there were three moms ahead of me—picking up their sons' corsages. As each corsage made their debut from the display case, we oohed and aahed in unison. I felt hopeful that this time would be different.

As I slipped to the front of the line, the florist with crinkling eyes smiled and asked, "Name, please?"

"Jonathan Pombo," I said with a grin.

I was almost giddy with excitement—as if it were my prom—until she laid the clear plastic corsage box on the counter.

No, not again, I thought. *It can't be!*

The corsage was a spring mix of red and yellow flowers (I ordered *pink!*). To make matters worse, it was a "pin-on" corsage —not a wristlet (Jenna's dress was *strapless!*). And there was a problem with the box. It was huge—almost coffinlike! The tiny corsage lay lifeless in a bed of fluorescent cellophane shreds.

A lump formed in my throat as I whimpered, "Excuse me, but I think this is the *wrong* corsage. In fact, I'm sure of it." The florist removed the pencil from behind her ear and checked the order sheet. "No, it says 'Pombo'—there's no mistake."

I stopped cringing long enough to take a closer look. *Maybe if it was in a smaller box, it wouldn't look so pitiful,* I thought.

As the florist rang up my purchase, I offered a suggestion, "Do you happen to have a smaller box?"

"Absolutely not!" she countered. "We're completely out of corsage boxes."

I reluctantly paid for the corsage and carried it to the car with a heavy heart. I needed to call Jon.

"Jon, there's a little problem with the corsage."

"Mom—it's okay—just come home."

As I drove up the long driveway to our house, Jon greeted me at the side entrance. He looked hopeful until I produced the container holding the lifeless corsage. "So what do you think?" I sniffled.

"I think it needs a smaller box."

I burst into tears, "No, not again. Can't it be 'perfect' just once?"

My mind raced—just two hours left. I could try the family-owned florist down the street. They always had a wide selection of flowers. *Why didn't I go there in the first place?*

"Jon, keep the corsage in the refrigerator until I get back," I shouted.

As I entered the small one-room florist shop, the door jingled, and the scent of roses wafted through the air.

"Excuse me, I'm in a hurry," I stammered. "You don't happen to have any prom corsages, do you? I need a pink one."

The florist glared at me and snapped, "No, we closed five minutes ago."

Back in the car, I called Jon while I fought back tears, "I'm driving downtown—keep the corsage cool."

"Mom, there's not enough time."

"Don't wait for me. I'll meet you at the church for pictures—I promise."

I threaded my way through traffic and practiced my opening line, "HELP ME!"

I swerved into the parking lot of the *third* florist—armed with a picture of Jenna's prom gown and a swatch of material from the hem of her dress.

As I approached the counter my voice trembled, "I need a pink prom corsage and you're my last hope."

Apologetically, the florist explained, "We're completely out of pink flowers, but someone just returned a corsage; I think it might be what you are looking for." The florist pointed to the main display case at the front of the store.

With tears clouding my eyes, I whispered, "Thank you!"

As I rounded the corner, there were green buckets filled with white carnations and daisies, but nothing in pink. And then, out of the corner of my eye—on the top shelf—a corsage box.

My heart pounded heavily as I reached for the box. To my delight, it was a wristlet corsage made up of seven sweetheart roses in pale pink. There was a ribbon of pearls, a sprig of baby's breath, and holly fern. It was perfect!

I glanced at my watch—twenty minutes to get to the church on time. I paid for the corsage and scampered out the door.

As I drove into the parking lot, I saw an ocean of limos and a sea of tuxes. *How would I ever find Jon?* I thought.

Then, out of nowhere, Jon appeared. The picture of the once-little boy—now a man with broad shoulders, standing tall and handsome—made me fight back tears. His boutonniere clumsily hung sideways as he reached out to hug me. I inwardly smiled, reveling in the moment.

"Mom, did you find something pink? I brought the other one just in case."

"There's no need, honey; look what I have."

Jon's green eyes sparkled with excitement, "Thanks, Mom!"

We walked to the reflecting pool where the formal pictures were being taken. Jenna looked like a princess, and together they complemented each other like a bride and groom on top of a wedding cake.

I watched expectantly as Jon placed the corsage on Jenna's wrist while I snapped the picture of a lifetime. She was smiling into his eyes and gasped, "Jon, it's absolutely perfect!"

With misty eyes, I followed them out to the limo and stood waving until they disappeared from sight.

I stayed up for Jon's return that night. It was a little past midnight when I heard the door close softly. I crept off the sofa and asked, "Jon, how was the prom?"

"It was okay. The dinner was cold, the room was hot, but Jenna loved her corsage!"

With a twinkle in his eye, he said, "Thanks, Mom, you did it again."

"No, Jon, God did it. He always works it out perfectly when we leave it in his hands!"

Mentoring
Moms

One Small Step

By Amy Mullis

I n 1969 I was in the fifth grade and tremendously impressed with myself. I was adept at Very Important Things—spelling, playing jacks, and begging to be allowed to wear panty hose. I was one of the first ones picked when we played Red Rover at recess. I was in control of my world. Except the panty hose thing. Mom controlled the market there, and she wasn't interested in negotiations.

The world outside saw many changes that year. Man walked on the moon for the very first time. I remember because Mom made me stop playing with my ironing board and my iron that really got hot (if 20 degrees below lukewarm counts as hot), to watch some man in a snowsuit bounce down a shadowy ladder onto a surface that was covered with more dust than you could find underneath my brother's bed. One small step.

I think it was the same year that the grown-ups started chattering about something else. They talked about busing kids to school. I didn't get it. Kids rode the bus to school every day and had done so throughout my vast years of school experience. Personally, I was not a bus rider. The only time I ever rode a school bus was on a field trip (and then I threw up).

Mom tried to explain that these were kids riding buses to schools that weren't in their neighborhoods, an idea that seemed decidedly odd to me. School was okay, but I felt sorry for any kid that had to spend any more time than necessary getting there and back. That sort of mileage would eat up valuable playtime.

I grew up in small-town South Carolina. There was one elementary school, one junior high (until it burned down), and one high school. The boundaries of my world held these things plus three churches, two dime stores located in the single-street location of small shops known simply as "town," and one fast-food place that had three stone tables outside where you could eat right there at the restaurant. All this talk about busing and neighborhoods didn't make sense. I can't say it didn't compute, because nothing computed back then, unless it was our tiny, overworked brains sweating over long division.

Then one day Mama explained something to me. I knew it must be something important because she used that "special" voice when she talked; the slow, clear voice that let me know she was serious, but that I wasn't in any trouble. I already knew that she always made sure to help me understand what was happening anytime I came across something that was new to me, and I hadn't reached the omniscience of teenage years, so I paid attention. Everything made sense when she used her practical Mary Poppins voice. Trouble was, she wasn't explaining anything that I hadn't already learned from her all through my life. Mom worked in a hardware store in town, and you could never tell if one customer was more important to her than another. She talked to everyone like they'd been friends for a very long time.

Now she used the word "integration" and said that I would have more children of different races in my class and that I might even have a teacher who wasn't white. I can remember her calm, matter-of-fact voice telling me, "Amy, never judge a person by how they look. You can't tell if people are good or bad just by looking at their skin or their clothes or their hair. You have to save room in your heart to look at them there. Besides, if someone judged you by how you look right now," she smiled, taking in my jelly-stained mouth and skinny, mud-streaked legs, "they might get the wrong idea about you."

Several of my friends left that year to go to private schools. Private school? It sounded slightly shady, if not downright illegal to me. "Some people are afraid of change. They panic when something is different, but they'll be back," Mama predicted. And the very next year, there they were, walking down the halls, complaining about homework, and giggling in the lunch line, just like always.

The details may be different—she didn't have to deal with video games or text messaging—but I think I stuck to Mama's principles when I raised my sons. Today I have kids that have friends of different races, religions, personalities, and preferences. I didn't realize until I had children of my own, who were studying history out of a slick, hardbound book, that my life is what history lessons are made of. I just lived the kind of life Mama taught me. One small step at a time.

Hey!
Kool-Aid Mom!

By Sandy Foster Brooks

"Oh, Yeah! Kool-Aid's here, bringing ya fun. Kool-Aid's got, thirst on the run. Get a big, wide, happy ear-to-ear Kool-Aid smi-i-ile. . . ." You remember the song! That Kool-Aid smile. Mom had that. The title "Kool-Aid Mom" was bestowed upon her by a neighborhood friend years after we'd grown up. My friend was right. Mom was the Kool-Aid Mom— zany, fun-loving, and full of energy. Brownies for breakfast? Yup. Fresh-baked cookies and milk after school? Nearly every day. Summer afternoons spent walking in the rain, searching for the end of a rainbow? Repeatedly. But as we grew up, Mom did, too.

Dad was an alcoholic. He walked out after twenty-six years of marriage, leaving her to raise four kids alone. She never said an ill word about him or any of his subsequent wives, nor would she let us kids. Choosing never to remarry, or even date for that matter, she wanted to devote her time to the thing she loved best: being a mom.

I learned many life lessons during the twenty years I had with her. Things like watching out for the underdog, putting a positive spin on life, not being too hard on yourself or others, and always, *always* persevering.

The summer of my sixteenth birthday provided me, as a young woman, an opportunity to witness yet another example of my incredible mom. It was hot that summer. Really hot. One of those Midwestern types of hot where the humidity drips off you and makes you feel as though you're breathing through a warm, moist washrag. Tempers flare and liquor flows on days like that.

This is how it was that Saturday. I'd driven to the next town over to visit Dad, my stepmom, Marilyn, and her daughter, Pam, who was my age. Pam and I had been waiting for this night for a long time! "Summer Jam!" Summer Jam was a concert venue where half a dozen of the country's hottest bands came to town, filling the local sports stadium with screaming young fans. Every teenager's dream outing! Our parents were supposed to take us that evening.

I arrived before lunch and noticed Dad and Marilyn were already drinking. This wasn't unusual, but I was somewhat concerned that if they didn't pace themselves, Pam and I would be hard-pressed to get to the concert later that night. Though we both could drive, neither of us relished the idea of getting on the interstate and traveling to the sports complex with some sixty thousand other concertgoers.

The drinking this day, however, did not lighten up. In fact, it continued to increase as the afternoon went by. Along with it, the petty arguments and bickering started in. Slurred words and accusations became the order of the day.

As things began to deteriorate, Pam and I went outside to escape the loud, angry voices that were escalating indoors. Even though it was incredibly hot, we welcomed the solitude of being outside. The only sound was the gentle humming of the neighbor's air conditioner.

I stared off into the distance. "So, what do you want to do?" I asked Pam. Neither of us wanted to speak the dreaded thought that we might not be going to the concert later that night.

"I dunno. What do you want to do?" she mumbled back.

"We could go down to Dwayne's house and see if he's home," I suggested. Dwayne was a kid our age who lived a few houses down. He was okay to hang around with. At that point in time, *anybody* would have been okay to hang around with.

"Sure. Let's go."

We started off down the street, the sun glaring down on us. Before we had gotten very far, loud, angry voices began to break the silence. As we turned and looked back, we saw Dad and Marilyn. Totally blitzed by now, they were in a standoff out in the front yard. Pam and I looked at each other completely aghast, totally embarrassed.

"What in the world?" I wondered aloud.

There was Dad, armed with a large lead-glass ashtray, and Marilyn had a knife. They were screaming at the top of their lungs, totally unaware of the scene they were causing. They paced around each other, somewhat shakily, like a couple of has-been boxers in a ring. Every now and then, one or the other of them would brandish their "weapon" at the other and hurl obscenities.

As the scene began to register in our minds, we heard the sound of sirens growing closer. Someone had called the police! Neither of us knew what to do. Our parents were completely out of control!

Pam and I exchanged a horrified look and, without speaking, quickly laid out our plan. She darted toward Dwayne's front door, looking for a place of escape. I cut through the side yard, ran around back, and waited, thankful that at least I had a safe, loving home to run to.

The officers arrived and quickly got things under control, relocating the argument indoors. That was my chance! I dashed to my car and made a beeline for home, the concert long forgotten.

I thought back over the day's events as I drove. Disappointed, but not surprised by what had happened, I could hardly wait to tell Mom.

"Mom? Mom, where are you?" I shouted as soon as I entered the little split-level house. I slammed the front door behind me.

"I'm in here! What's wrong, for heaven's sake?" she hollered back.

I rushed to the cheery yellow kitchenette, cheeriness being the last thing on my mind.

"Mom, you won't believe what they did!" The words spilled out in a frantic jumble. "I've never been so embarrassed in my life!"

Afraid of who "they" were, yet knowing deep down exactly who I was referring to, Mom asked, "You mean your dad and Marilyn? What have they done now?"

Mom had watched as the years since their divorce unfolded. Always in the background, always quietly. Through the unprovoked phone calls she received from a drunken Marilyn, through the drive-by drunken obscenities shouted at our house at dinnertime, through it all. Never an embittered word spoken, never a scathing remark well placed. She maintained her composure and her pride.

Immediately I began to blurt out the whole thing. I told her about the drinking, the arguing, and the sordid sparring match in the front yard, complete with "referees."

"Oh, my gosh!" came her reply, as she sat down absently on a bright yellow kitchen chair. Her blue eyes locked on mine.

"Where is Pam? Is she at home? She doesn't need to be pulled into that!"

"No. She went to Dwayne's house, I think."

"Well, your father and Marilyn are going to have quite a night, I'd say. Someone may even end up in jail over this. Who knows what might happen . . ." her words trailed off, as if thinking out loud about all of the possible ramifications of the day's events.

She sat there in silence for a while, staring off, contemplating her choices, her opportunity to make a difference.

"Sandy, I want you to drive back over there and see if you can find Pam," she said. "Make sure she's all right, and tell her she is welcome to spend the night here if she would like. That child has no business being caught up in something like this."

At sixteen, I thought that was really cool. Mom was offering to let Pam stay with us until things calmed down at her house. I knew if I could find her, she would very much want to come to our house. Pam knew of Mom from my stories, from hearing my dad speak of her, and from my brother and sisters. Now she would get to meet her and learn for herself what a special person she was.

I found Pam hiding. She did indeed want to come with me that night. We sneaked past the police and headed for home. She ended up spending several days with us, until her dad heard what happened and offered to take her in.

At sixteen, I thought what Mom did was pretty "kool." At forty-six, it's even "kooler." I learned a lot that day, but most of it didn't sink in until years later. She took in the other woman's child. She opened her heart, though it had often been hurt. She opened her home with love and acceptance, with no place for bitterness or unforgiveness.

We had about four more years with Mom before she died from breast cancer at fifty-four. Her funeral was attended by people of all ages and walks of life, people that I didn't even know. Yes, she was loved by many, because she loved all.

♡

Teatime

By Linda Kaullen Perkins

Often, when I was growing up, I walked into the kitchen about the time Mama was standing at the white granite sink filling the silver teakettle. I might go back into the next room and pretend to be interested in my dolls, but I was really waiting to hear the first squeal of the teakettle's whistle. In moments like that—moments of anticipation—life's pleasures become as defined and intense as a heartbeat through a stethoscope.

When cups and saucers clattered as Mama pulled them from the cabinet, I could stand it no longer but felt compelled to join her at the kitchen table. I knew the ritual well, yet never grew tired of it, just as one never tires of receiving a fat envelope with a handwritten letter or an unexpected compliment from a stranger.

"You may use this first," she'd say, filling the hinged silver spoon with dried tea leaves. I got napkins, the cookie jar, and the sugar bowl, but it still seemed an eternity before the teakettle's whistle reached the right pitch. Then ribbons of steam rose from my cup as Mama poured the scalding water. I clutched the spoon, dunking and swirling it, and refused to let go. The holey spoon sent spirals of darkness into my white Hopalong Cassidy mug.

"Is it enough yet, Mama?" I'd ask when the water held a hint of stain.

"Be patient, dear. All good things take time," she'd say.

I'd dip a clean spoon into the sugar bowl and pull it out rounded with white crystals. She would shake her head. "Not that much." I'd brush off a few grains. Then, without hesitation, I dumped the sweetness into the tea before she had a chance to say any more.

I would lift the mug to my lips and feel the heat radiating from it. "Be careful," she would warn. "Better blow on it first." Again, I should have been patient, but I couldn't wait. With my first sip, I often squealed, "Ouch!" The scalding liquid paralyzed my tongue with a numbing sensation.

"Let it sit a minute," she warned, preparing her own cup of tea. "Go get your deck of cards and I'll play one game with you."

Burned tongue forgotten, I would run to the chest of drawers and pull out the card box labeled "Authors," my favorite game. Even before I knew I wanted to be a writer, facts about famous writers fascinated me. I memorized their works and planned to read them when I was older.

Cards flashed as she shuffled them with nimble fingers, while her cup of tea grew darker than the walnut fruit bowl sitting on the counter. "You may go first," she would say, before removing the spoon and sipping her tea.

I studied my cards before asking, "Do you have Sir Walter Scott?"

"Hmmm." She pulled out a card and handed it to me. "I just read something about him yesterday. He lived in Scotland in a house near the Tweed River." She took another sip of tea. "I can't remember the name of the town, but it was Mel something. Anyway, Scotland is a place where they drink tea often."

"They do?" I looked at my cup of tea with new appreciation. I pressed the mug to my lips and drew in a bit of the liquid. Its sweet warmth was almost as good as the cotton candy I begged for at Liberty Park.

"Imagine that," she said with a faraway look in her eyes. I knew she was going to tell me about a place we would probably never visit. "People clear across the ocean are sitting down and drinking tea, too." Her words and the tone of her voice painted vivid pictures in my mind, better than a high-powered telescope could focus an image.

"You think they are right now, Mama?" I felt a kinship to those people who enjoyed the same beverage I was sipping.

"I wouldn't be surprised. It's not morning there, but someone in Scotland is probably having a cup of tea right now."

I put my cards down and took another gulp of the warm liquid. The very idea of someone in a faraway, mysterious place drinking the same thing I was drinking seemed impossible to my young mind. I picked up the pair of cards with pictures of Sir Walter Scott. "You think he had tea, too?" I asked.

"I wouldn't be at all surprised," she said, as she reached for one of the cards. "Let me see it. Yes, right here. It lists his novels. He may have had a cup of tea when he was writing *Ivanhoe* or *Lady of the Lake*."

Today I think about those special times with Mama. She exhibited love, patience, tolerance, a thirst for knowledge, and compassion, and all of this occurred while we were drinking tea.

As a young girl I didn't know Mama was preparing me for life. I hope I possess those characteristics that were second nature to Mama.

I have put Mama's lessons to work many times. As an educator, I needed patience to work successfully with children and an abundance of patience to be a writer. One time I sold a story to a magazine and it took seven years to see it in print.

Now every morning when I have my cup of tea alone, I cherish moments of quiet reflection, my dreams surfacing and bobbing like life preservers on the ocean. Sometimes I think I hear Mama say, "Be patient, dear. All good things take time."

Terror in the Barnyard

By Minnie Browne

F or days, torrents of rain fell upon an already soaked land. Bayou Meto's currents raged over the banks, rushing angrily through the woods and into the barnyard. The gloominess from the weather hovered like a heavy fog over the farm.

This condition was compounded by Daddy's battle for his life. Momma's face could not hide her concern and fear from us. The words of Dr. Mitchell weighed heavily on her heart: "Mrs. Nordin, if Mr. Nordin lives, his heart can be severely damaged from the rheumatic fever." He was confined to his bed and completely unaware of what was happening around him.

With eight children still at home, Momma relied heavily on the older ones to help with the responsibilities of the farm and home. The first child, Lucille, was married and lived in Kansas. She wanted to be with us and help Momma, but it was impossible at that time. The third child, Ruth, was married and lived a short distance from us.

On this particular day, as daylight slipped into darkness, we completed our evening meal discussing the day's events in anxious, hushed voices. As Momma got up from the table, she took off her cotton print apron, carefully folded it, and put it aside.

She spoke softly, "Juanita, you, Owana, and Betty clear the table and do the dishes. Mary, you and Minnie go out to the pump and get some water . . . we need more for tonight."

Bennie and Joe finished all their chores and took our younger brother, Don, into the living room to listen to their favorite radio program, *The Shadow.*

"Mary, do you believe Daddy will get well?" I asked as we walked out of the circle of faint light into the deep darkness of the backyard to the pump. I was looking for some assurance from my older sister.

Mary thoughtfully replied, "I believe God will answer our prayers, and he will help Daddy get well. Come on—we need to hurry." I put the bucket on the pump spout and held it still while Mary pumped the water in.

The horses and mules started moving in the barnyard, making nervous whinnies. Then, the horrible, strange low noise—a combination of snorting and growling—broke through the sound of sloshing water as the horses and mules were now bucking, kicking, rearing up, and moving frantically in the dark.

"Mary, what is it?"

"I don't know! Let's get back to the house!"

"Momma! Momma! There is something in the barnyard! It's making horrible sounds!" We were both speaking excitedly.

"Shhh, Shhhh, don't let your daddy hear this," Momma said reassuringly as she tried to calm our fears.

"Bennie! Joe! Get the flashlight! You will have to see what is scaring the horses and mules. Mary, you and Minnie run and get

Alfred and have him bring his gun," Momma exclaimed as she initiated a plan of action.

Juanita, Owana, and Betty were trying to finish the dishes. They became very shaken by what they heard and continued trying to keep Don calm. They had to keep everything quiet so Daddy would not try to get up and help.

"Mary, don't run so fast." I was terrified. The hair on my neck stood up on end. I could feel the animal behind us—about to reach out and grab me, since I was slower. My imagination controlled my thoughts.

Ruth and Alfred lived a short distance up the road. Finally, we were at the door calling, "Alfred! Ruth! Something is scaring the horses and mules. It is making horrible noises. Bring the gun. Bennie and Joe are going out there!"

Immediately, we ran back to the house. Alfred joined Bennie and Joe as they walked to the barnyard. Ruth took us into the house. We waited anxiously for a gunshot as fear gripped us. As they approached the fence, the low snorting, growling noises continued.

"Do you see it?" Alfred asked.

"I hear it over there!" Bennie reported as he flashed the light in that direction.

"It sounds like it's walking on two feet." The darkness made it difficult to see with the animals running wild.

"There! Over there! Hear it?" Joe shouted intensely.

Bennie flashed the dim light in that direction. All of a sudden, they got a quick glimpse of a big, black, furry animal as it dropped to its four feet and ran through the water in the barnyard

back into the flooded woods. Alfred, Bennie, and Joe stayed by
the fence until the horses and mules calmed down.

"It looked like a black bear," Bennie told Momma. "We only
got a glimpse of a large black animal, but we heard it walking on
two feet and saw it drop to all four feet as it ran away." We sat
in the living room talking softly about the incident. We concluded it was a black bear, and the floodwaters caused it to leave
the deeper woods farther down the bayou in search of food and
dry land.

Momma helped us to successfully keep all the terror involved
in the barnyard event that night from Daddy until he got well.
Her faith in God and her love and concern for us guided us
through Daddy's illness, the flood, and the crisis with the bear.

♡

Detours of Life

By Helen Colella

Mom worked as a waitress at the corner luncheonette; her hours correlated with my school schedule. She made decent tips that helped pay the bills. Even at age seven I knew she came home exhausted and weary after a long day, but she never complained and just jumped into her other job—being a mother. She'd get dinner, do laundry, help us with homework, and do all the other chores surrounding a family.

One night a loud, frantic banging on our front door seemed to signal an emergency. A family friend brought the bad news that my father, Pep, had collapsed at Iggy's, the local tavern, and had been transported to City Hospital. Mom quickly sent us to my aunt's house and accepted the friend's offer to drive her to the hospital.

Dad had been ailing for several months, but we all believed his tiredness, coughing up blood, and rapid weight loss were attributed to his long overtime hours, irregular eating habits, and smoking. Then, as the symptoms intensified, Mom finally convinced him to agree to go for medical assistance. Unfortunately, it was too late.

When Mom returned home from the hospital that night, we learned that there was much more to his illness. Dad had been diagnosed with an advanced case of tuberculosis and the prognosis was grim. "He waited too long before seeking out help. All we can do now is admit him to the hospital where they can make him as comfortable as possible. The doctor says he's only got weeks left." Mom's tears of sadness flowed freely.

This was scary news for all of us. How did this happen? How could God allow it?

How would we survive?

My mother never expected to become a "single mom" in such a short period, but she had the foresight to prepare. During the nine weeks Dad lingered, she readied herself for his inevitable death, evaluated her needs, and made plans for herself and their two children. She signed up for a three-month night course that reviewed secretarial skills, rented a typewriter, and canvassed the businesses around our neighborhood looking for employment.

For nine weeks she juggled her waitress job, hospital visits, night school, and us kids, thinking of nothing but losing her husband and the welfare of her children. She fought off the devastation and depression that descended upon her with a powerful determination that I hoped would be passed down through the chromosomes.

It didn't take Mom long before she found a job with a decent starting salary within walking distance of our home. The hours of employment again matched school time, and the job would be available as soon as she finished her night class.

"Life is full of detours," Mom told everyone. "All we can do is make the best of what comes our way." Her simple, yet clear philosophy explained her outlook on how she would face the future.

At thirty-six, Mom's experience with death forced her into a new world—one of being a single working mother with a new set of rules, responsibilities, and values for the future, for her and her children. She accepted the challenge with dignity and proceeded without slowing down or complaining. "God will give me what I need."

Over the years that followed, Mom worked hard, often struggling to make ends meet, but she never gave up. Somehow she managed to keep a roof over our heads and keep us clothed and fed. Her deep faith confirmed the inner strength that God had bestowed upon her.

Several years passed before I developed the same symptoms as my father, and I was also diagnosed with tuberculosis and sent to an isolation hospital, which was part of the standard treatment in the 1950s. Again, Mom's tears of sadness flowed freely. How did this happen? How could God allow it, again? How would she survive if she lost her daughter?

This time, however, there wasn't a grim prognosis. "Childhood strains of this disease can be easily treated," the doctor assured her. "We caught it early enough for a successful healing and recovery. It may take a year, but your daughter will be healthy and lead a normal, productive life."

Mom tells us she heard the words, but her worst fear surfaced and overshadowed the prognosis. Only one question plagued her that she needed God to answer: "Will I lose my child as I did my husband?"

For months Mom did nothing but pray for my recovery: in stores, at work, in church, or just walking about, anywhere and everywhere. Anticipating another loss devastated her, yet somehow she managed to keep her job intact and her family functioning. During this time she struggled to find the inner strength she had possessed earlier in her life, her treasured gift from God.

I did recover and was released from the hospital after a year and a half: six months in isolation, medication, bed rest, and medical TLC. Joy consumed her being. Mom said, "I wasn't ready for this detour. It tested my faith and I should have remembered that God would unfold his plan as he saw fit."

From that point on, nothing ever seemed to be a problem for her; life continued along the same path: hard work, a daily struggle to make ends meet, and being able to take pleasure in and from her family. She managed to put us through college, save for retirement, and enjoy her grandchildren for years. Then, once again, she came face-to-face with another health detour. Her diagnosis turned out to be a respiratory illness—not tuberculosis but emphysema. The doctor's prognosis was grim: "It's not promising."

This time, no tears of sadness flowed. This time, she understood. This time, she didn't question God. In her final days she accepted her fate with a simple expression of faith: "God has completed his life plan for me. This is one detour I'm ready for."

Mom did her best to survive, provide for her family, and accept the detours that befell her. She modeled a way of life for me: accept challenge, do your best, and move forward.

Mama Left Her Handprint

By Linda O'Connell

O ur family didn't have the luxury of owning an electric fan in the early 1950s. On sweltering summer days, Mom would make a pallet for my brother and me, both preschoolers, by the front screen door. Napping was a reprieve from the unbearable heat. The midday sun hung heavy in the sky, and the humidity made the fibers from the thin sheet-blanket cling to our sweaty, shirtless little bodies. Mom wiped our faces with a wet cloth, then knelt between us and alternately rubbed our backs and fanned us with a *Look* magazine. The slight breeze and her gentle caress were soothing, and despite the heat, we drifted off to sleep listening to her favorite serial soap opera playing on the radio, *Young Dr. Malone*.

After our naps and a full day of active outdoor play, Mom would bathe us and put us to bed as the sun went down. After she said our bedtime prayers with us and talked about right from wrong, she and Dad would sit in front of the big wooden floor-model Philco radio and listen to the *Jack Benny Program*. I laughed right along with them. Even though I didn't understand the humorous exchanges between Jack Benny and his gravelly voiced sidekick, Rochester, I enjoyed the laughter that filled our home each evening right before I drifted off to sleep.

One of Mom's greatest lessons was about telling a lie. I failed to comprehend the nuances as she explained that a white lie was different from a blatant lie. She said that sometimes people told little fibs that were much different from outright, deliberate lies. She gave examples, such as if someone asks if you think her dress is pretty, and you don't think so, it's okay to smile and nod. A little white lie sometimes protects the other person's feelings, she explained. I insisted that I would always tell the truth. And I did.

On one particular occasion, my truth telling actually created a problem for Mom. She spied the life insurance man coming up the walk to collect his weekly premium, and because she didn't have the money to pay him, she panicked and did the unthinkable. She asked me to tell a lie. "Listen, honey, I'm going to step out the back door, and I want you to tell the insurance collector that I'm not here. Ask him to come back on Friday, and tell him I'll pay him then. Can you do that for me?" I shook my banana curls fiercely. "No, Mama, I can't tell a lie." I was almost five, and I knew better. My moral compass was pointed in the right direction; she'd aimed it!

"Listen, honey, I really won't be in here, so it's not a lie; it's just one of those tiny little fibs. This is one of those times when it is okay." I looked into her pleading eyes and evaluated my situation. Whose feelings was I protecting—the insurance man's or Mom's?

"Can you do it or not? You know you're my little trooper." She patted my hair as she headed out the back door. I nodded and smiled, seeking Mom's approval. I wanted to please her, yet I wanted to do the right thing. It didn't feel right either way, but I did my best.

When the insurance man, who knew our family very well, rapped at the screen door, I greeted him with a wide smile and heavy heart. I looked him straight in the face and said, "My mama told me to tell you she's not home and to come back on Friday to collect the insurance money."

"Really?" he belly laughed. "Okay, come on out, Virginia, your little girl just told on you."

Mom walked to the door embarrassed, shot me "the look," and then apologized to the agent. They had a laugh and a cup of coffee. "Yeah, she's my little trooper," Mom told the man as she patted me on the head. I couldn't figure out if being her little trooper was a bad or good thing. It was hard to tell from her expression and the way her eyebrows rose way up under her bangs when she looked at me.

Mom wasn't perfect and neither was I. That night as she listened to me say my prayers, she apologized for her actions and told me that I had handled the situation well. I'd done the right thing. Was I relieved!

I told the brutal truth from then on. When Grandma asked, "What did your mama say about the meat loaf I sent?" I answered bluntly, "She said, 'Yuck' and gave it to Daddy."

"That's my little trooper," Mom said and tousled my hair when Grandma confronted her about my revelation.

When the neighbor lady came for a visit and asked me what my mom was doing, I replied honestly, "Going potty."

"That's my little trooper," Mom said with an embarrassed expression.

I trooped with her from one house to the next when she visited neighbors. Mom knew she could always count on me to give an accurate account of their lives to Dad when he came home and asked what we'd done all day.

"That's my little trooper," Mom would smile and pat my bottom as she shooed me out the door. Mom passed away recently, but I will never forget her words of wisdom and her loving touch. Mom left her legacy in the form of her handprint on my head, her imprinted moral messages on my heart, and her gentle fingertip strokes all over her little trooper's back.

♡

Lessons in Grace

By Patricia Hoyt

S he sits alone in her wheelchair, the constant *whoosh* of the oxygenator providing a lulling background amid the busyness of the skilled nursing facility. These used to be called nursing homes, but for the baby boomers this evoked awful smells, unanswered calls for assistance, and lonely people, so the name has been changed. Regardless of the name change, the lonely elderly still live there.

I have flown from far away, driven two hours, and have arrived exhausted. Peeking around the door of her room, I quietly observe an elderly woman, hair straight, chin dropped to her chest, breathing to the rhythm of the sound in the room. I recheck the number on the door, but as I look more closely, my heart breaks and tears flow, as I realize it's really my mother I'm looking at. I walk in slowly, not knowing whether I want to wake her. I know she will smile, tell me how great I look, and thank me for coming. And the guilt I feel will be overwhelming.

But I do wake her and we catch up on the news of my husband, our travels, and our lives in another state. I ask her about her days, but she says they're all pretty much the same, although she's happy here. I know she lies for my sake and probably for hers, because with her deep health issues, there are no other choices.

And so, you see, my mother is the most courageous woman I know. In spite of the limited circumstances of her life, she maintains an enthusiastic and eager outlook about those around her. She has never made me feel guilty for not seeing her more; she's just glad for the moment. She drinks in information about my life (even though the next day we will repeat the same sentences). She loves to go anywhere, in spite of the oxygen tank that follows her wheelchair.

I have learned many lessons about how to age with grace and dignity, and how to make those around you want to be around you. Heroes are often thought of as being physically strong and able to perform amazing feats, but my mother's courage puts them to shame. In her weakness she has shown the kind of strength that comes from the deep love she has for those she cares for and from the moral character that is not celebrated in our newspapers or on our televisions.

♡

Observations from a Mom

By Cynthia Thrift

1. Never stand directly over your potty-training child. They jump to their feet in full force without warning and knock your jaw out of alignment.

2. Do not under any circumstance spell these words: t-o-y-s, i-c-e c-r-e-a-m, or c-a-n-d-y. Infants and toddlers spell before they speak in *any language*.

3. Mumbling incoherently under your breath is clearly audible to children, and they will repeat it at the most awkward moments, like in church, during a meeting, or in front of new friends.

4. Children have no poker face.

5. Grabbing private areas to dance provocatively regardless of the "stop it now" looks you shoot them is normal. You honestly have no idea where they saw this; they just knew how to do it.

6. Girls and boys will blurt out ridiculously embarrassing names for genitalia even though you *never* use silly terms to explain anatomy. You give them the correct biological term and they come up with the nicknames. They really do.

7. Kids point out others' flaws at a volume that everyone hears and that echoes to the Great Wall of China, where it bounces back and is repeated.

8. There is no quiet, inside voice.

9. No matter the area of space surrounding you, children will stomp and clobber your bare feet while walking by or when attempting to reach you. Every time.

10. A closed bathroom door means nothing. You need their help.

11. A pink plastic T-ball bat and Wiffle ball does hurt.

12. Babies and toddlers secretly sharpen their fingernails and know the tender spots on which to practice the claw grip.

13. The seventh dimension exists. You know it does because the match to the shoe you're missing is there, along with the remote, fresh packs of unopened batteries, and your favorite earrings.

14. Freak viruses that produce projectile vomit only happen the night before a big day.

15. Your children will remain unscathed and unbruised until two minutes before you walk into the scheduled photography studio. Bruises and Band-Aids, preferably on the nose, will magically appear.

16. The most important observation of all? All children are fantastic!

Simple Lessons

By Ava Pennington

y favorite life lessons have come from unusual sources, including Bambi, a box of Valentine's Day chocolates, and a pinch of salt—not what you might consider to be typical educational tools.

The oldest of three daughters, my teenage and young adult years were spent, in part, pondering a question familiar to most young people: how could my sheltered mother, who barely graduated high school, teach me more than I could learn in college, graduate school, and later in the corporate world?

After all, Mom immigrated to this country as a teenager and didn't attend college, while I went on to complete graduate school and receive an M.B.A. in executive management. She hadn't worked outside the home for more than fifty years and didn't even have a driver's license. I'm a career woman who worked as an executive for several international financial companies. What could she possibly have contributed to my education? I was sure that she was the one who had much to learn. But, in fact, I discovered that Mom had taught me a great deal more than I realized. I'm still learning, and memories have been some of my best professors.

My first lessons were not in a classroom, but rather at home sitting next to Mom, mesmerized as she read of Bambi's innocence, Cinderella's romance, and Aladdin's magic lamp. She read of marvelous worlds, her voice animated in lilting, hushed, excited, or somber tones, and I hung on to every word with bated breath. Even after I learned to read, I still enjoyed the special treat of sitting by her side and following her into those extraordinary places concealed between the binders. These times contributed to my love of reading.

Our visits to the neighborhood library were like trips to a treasure chest—so many choices! Mysterious and fascinating worlds waited to be explored, and I held the passport in my hands: my very own library card. If the maximum number of books that one could borrow was six, then six I took, devoured them, and returned for more.

One time, however, I borrowed a book that I didn't enjoy. Although I set it aside after the first few pages, Mom had her own ideas. She required that I finish what I had started—how cruel I considered her to be! I completed the other five books and picked up the offensive tome with reluctance. I read it grudgingly, and in spite of myself became captivated with the turn of each page. I ended up loving it! But more than just enjoying a novel, I learned something else—the value of self-discipline and perseverance.

Then there was the time Mom tried to teach me the alphabet in her native language. *Alif, baa, taa, thaa* . . . She worked hard not to laugh, but I could see the corners of her mouth turned up at the way her New York City born-and-bred daughter pronounced sounds as familiar to her as the ABCs were to me. I never did become conversant in her first language (my loss), but I went on to learn both French and Spanish, my respect for other languages and cultures having been nurtured in those early years.

While I enjoyed reading mysteries, working out a real-life puzzle was much more fun. Every year I looked forward to solving the annual Chocolate Mystery. Dad would bring Mom a large heart-shaped box of chocolates each Valentine's Day. What little (and not-so-little) girl hasn't gazed into a box of chocolates, wondering which ones were the "good" ones? They all looked delicious, but one bite might result in ecstasy (in my case, cherry or caramel) or regret (coconut). Mom, however, possessed the amazing ability to pick out the "right" chocolates time after time. She was practically infallible! And little by little, she would encourage us to try new flavors. I learned more than just how to pick out chocolates (a critical skill in life that I have since come to greatly appreciate). I also learned how to be observant and not to be afraid of trying new things.

Mom had a reputation for being a fantastic cook, a skill I looked forward to developing. But in junior high school, my home economics teacher (the "expert") stressed the importance of following recipes to the letter, including precise measurement of all ingredients. Yet there was Mom—a pinch of this and a toss of that. And there I was, trying to explain to Mom how important it was to *measure*! Since Mom's results were delicious nearly every time, I began to wonder if my teachers did *not* know more than Mom in *every* subject.

Mom shared our joys and disappointments, and took pride in

our accomplishments—both big and small. Her daughters are all grown and married now, and she and Dad are enjoying retirement. The older I get, the more I appreciate all that Mom is and all that she has given us.

Thanks, Mom, from a daughter who still has a lot more to learn.

♡

My Other Mothers

By Ellen Javernick

I never sent them Mother's Day cards, but they were also my mentors and role models. Each of these women has, in her own way, influenced my life.

Aunt Doll was really my great-aunt, old already in my childhood memories. A big-boned, stern-looking spinster, she wore housedresses and hairnets to do her housework. She lived alone above my uncle's law office in the small South Dakota town where we spent our summers. She expected good table manners and hearty appetites for the "farmer's meals" she fixed. We never had the nerve to say no to the gluey, lumpy oatmeal she insisted we share if we arrived before she'd eaten breakfast.

Her pioneer father, proud of the state he'd helped settle, named her Dollie Dakota. It suited her. To our chagrin, she clung to the ways of the Old West by using a chamber pot. Needless to say, we didn't beg to stay overnight! But we did stop by to visit every day. Aunt Doll had no children's toys. Instead she let us use her knick-knacks to create elaborate, imaginary worlds. On various occasions, her brass candlesticks became the sole source of light in our card table "sod house" or the ship's lantern on the sofa schooner.

On hot summer afternoons she served us Squirt, the sweet-sour grapefruity drink that made our mouths pucker. She was never too busy to play cards, canasta being her favorite. With her help the youngest of the cousins won more than his share of the games, but we didn't complain.

With Aunt Doll we didn't dare complain. She wouldn't have tolerated it. Besides, she didn't complain, despite the fact (we were told in hushed whispers) that her fiancé ran off and married someone else. She didn't complain when she had to sell the family farm or when the doctors had to amputate her cancerous leg. When I'm tempted to complain about small things, I try to remember the courage she showed when she accepted God's plan for her life.

Aunt Isabelle was another single lady. By then unmarried women weren't called spinsters. She taught art at Ohio University —and she painted nudes! We giggled about it behind her back. Of course, our parents picked a landscape rather than a naked lady for our living room. A perfectionist as well as a painter, Aunt Isabelle measured the distance between the broiler and the steak and chose a single perfect flower instead of a bouquet. Her clothes were prim and practical. Her shoes were what writers described as "sturdy." She never owned a bathing suit and bought her first and only pair of pants so she could ride on a llama in Nepal. She sent us postcards from the most exciting places: Africa, when she went there as a member of the very first Peace Corps group, and Antarctica, where she celebrated her eightieth birthday. We thought she was poor, and it was only after her death that we discovered that she'd been as careful about picking stocks as she was about picking perfect grapes from the grocery store. When she didn't need something, she didn't buy it. Instead, she saved the money—well over a million dollars—to share in the form of art scholarships to the university. When I'm tempted to buy things I don't need, I am reminded of her example, and I look for ways I, too, can share.

When I married, I acquired additional aunts, amazing ladies all! There was Aunt Josephine. Her old-fashioned name suited her. A tiny lady, she had more energy than the Energizer Bunny. Since she couldn't have children, and adoption wasn't an often-considered option for poor folks during the Depression, she borrowed my husband. Each morning after Uncle Frank headed off to the coal mine, his namesake, Little Frankie, arrived, lunch bucket in hand to help Aunt Josephine hunt for eggs. Then he'd perch on the big stool in the kitchen to keep her company while she cooked—and did she ever cook: donuts, dumplings, and crunchy, crusty loaves of bread. She cooked all the traditional Slovenian dishes, too—without recipes. She was a first-generation American citizen and proud of it. Each November she donned her best sunbonnet, the one with the yellow flowers, and went off to the local school to serve as an election judge. When I'm tempted to take our country's freedoms for granted, I think of Aunt Josephine. Maybe my one vote will matter. Maybe my letter to the editor will make a difference.

Aunt Marge lived in the little house next door to Grandma's. Soon after they moved in, Uncle Joey converted their garage into a beauty shop. All the older Italian ladies went there for a weekly shampoo and set. They picked Marge's instead of the fancy salons downtown because she could understand them even when they lapsed into the language of the old country. She listened with interest as they discussed the best way to make gnocchi, the troubles Junior was having with his teacher, or whether the church really needed a new addition. As successful as any psychologist, she allowed them to talk out their problems in their personal lives. When she retired, she took on the job of looking after Grandma. Her efforts weren't always appreciated. Sometimes the tomatoes she picked at the market weren't firm enough, the only parking place at the doctor's office wasn't close enough, or the piece of cake she brought over was too rich. Marge never discontinued her daily visits, despite the fact that they meant she'd have to listen to how Grandma was feeling, which was usually not good. When my husband apologized for Grandma's crotchetiness, Marge reminded us that God never promised we'd be praised for helping others. When I'm tempted to pout because I've not been thanked for a kindness, I think of Aunt Marge and her example of unselfish service.

Shirley joined our family after her first husband died. She took care of Great-Grandma at the nursing home and fell in love with Uncle Eddie, a gentle giant of a man who for years had cared for Great-Grandma himself. I can remember how delighted the family was when, at last, he married her. He deserved a good woman, they said. And Shirley was a good woman. Just ten years later Uncle Eddie was diagnosed with Parkinson's disease. Cheerfully, never patronizingly, Shirley helped him dress. She took over his chores and fed him his meals. As his illness progressed, she continued to treat him with dignity. She ignored his tremors and calmed his fears. When I'm occasionally annoyed because my husband has trouble hearing, I try to think of Shirley and her commitment to the part of the marriage vow that says "in sickness and in health." Because of Shirley's example, I try to be more accepting of others' weaknesses and to thank God for my many blessings.

The greeting card companies don't let us forget our mothers and mothers-in-law and even our grandmothers. Maybe they are missing a market. Maybe they should sell cards for the other women in our lives, the women, who by their example encourage us to be the best we can be.

The Power of Positive Thought

By Jacqueline Seewald

I f there's anyone who can teach and inspire positive thinking, it's my husband's mother. At ninety-three years of age, she's still physically active and mentally sharp. She could easily write her own book on the power of positive thought, but she does not pay lip service to the philosophy; she simply lives it.

Lillian told me a story about herself that is indicative of the kind of indomitable person she is. When my husband was small and his brother and sister were just babies, the family was quite poor. Lillian's brother David had married into a prominent Midwestern family. Unexpectedly, David's in-laws came East, and he brought them around to his sister's apartment to introduce them. Lillian met a well-dressed, white-haired lady wearing white gloves and a hat accompanied by an impressively tall air force general. Lillian was wearing a shabby housedress upon which one of the babies had spit up. Diapers hung from rope lines through their railroad flat. But what could have been embarrassing for everyone turned into a cheerful occasion. Undaunted, my mother-in-law welcomed her impressive guests into the crowded apartment and made them feel right at home with her warmth and friendliness.

"We're so pleased to meet you. What can I get for you?" she said. "We have coffee, tea, or juice. Please come into the kitchen and sit down."

With that, all awkwardness quickly disappeared. Lillian was a gracious hostess. There were homemade treats always ready in her kitchen. (Lillian has always been an exceptional baker.) Her homey touches make people—rich and poor alike—feel comfortable.

Lillian doesn't get sick; the word "illness" is not in her vocabulary. That may seem unrealistic to most of us, but it works for her. She believes in the power of the mind to heal; that most illness can be overcome or made better with the right sort of thinking. She considers herself a healthy human being.

Laid low by abnormal bleeding, she found out that she had a tumor. The doctors were convinced she had cancer. She refused to accept or believe the diagnosis, but she agreed to have the operation performed. My husband was pleasantly surprised to see her alert and eager to sit up soon after surgery. The doctors were amazed.

My husband's father had Parkinson's disease and suffered with it for seventeen years. After they retired from productive jobs, my in-laws traveled, went square dancing regularly, and belonged to the YMCA, where they swam almost daily. It was hard on both of them to give up such enjoyable activities. However, because of Lillian's positive attitude, her husband did not give up on life. He remained as active as he possibly could. It was a struggle for him every day, but he and Lillian viewed it only as another of life's challenges. There were no such things as tears or self-pity in either of their lexicons. They thought only about living, not dying.

Lillian puts the best possible spin on things. Her glass is always full. She sees the best in other people, never criticizes or looks for imperfections, compliments whenever possible, and simply won't give in to negative thinking. I once asked her how she manages to do this so consistently, because her life, like that of the rest of us, has had its share of grief and losses. This was her response: "When things start to look bad to me, I go out and treat myself to something I really like. It might be an ice-cream soda, or a hot fudge sundae, or a chocolate bar. I don't worry about the calories. It might be a special sweater or dress. I make a point not to look at the price tag at that time. And then I just seem to feel a lot better. Every morning that I wake up is a gift I've been given. Every new morning is the chance for something good to happen in my life, the chance for me to do something good with my life. I remind myself how great it is just to be alive."

Lillian is always interested in other people. She is generous to charities. She keeps in touch with her grandchildren and great-grandchildren as well as her children. She recently finished knitting hats and sweaters for the two newest great-grandchildren.

She never forgets a birthday, anniversary, or holiday gift for each of us. She is also interested in her friends and neighbors, as well as keeping informed on what is happening in the world. She is an avid reader and listens to radio and TV. Lillian intends to learn how to use a computer next and is learning new cable patterns for her knitting. She never stops or gives up on life. She is still trying out new recipes and still the best baker I know.

It would have been easy to give in to depression when the parents she loved died, or even worse, when her youngest son passed away of a brain tumor, having just really started his career as a doctor. But she never gave in to feelings of grief. She and Dad cared for him with every bit of love and energy they possessed until the day he died. When my husband's father finally passed away, she suffered. But now she remembers only the love and good times they shared together.

"He was the best husband a woman could have," she tells me.

Lillian now spends a lot of time at a senior center in her city where many courses are offered that keep her mind and body active. She takes a course in Shakespeare and is learning how to paint landscapes. She's friendly with another lady who, at 105, still enjoys playing bridge at the center.

I love visiting my mother-in-law because she is an inspiration to the rest of us. I hope to live the rest of my life with as much grace and dignity as she has. What she has to teach us all is that life is full of possibilities.

Memories
of Mom

The Valentine Sweetheart

By Terri Elders

> To dance is to be out of yourself.
> Larger, more beautiful, more powerful.
>
> —AGNES DE MILLE

As a nurse escorted her to the center of the recreation room, I remembered Mama's insistence that she'd been born dancing. "I tapped right on Mother's tummy," she'd joke. I'd seen photos of her preteen self in tap shoes or tutus, but I never could coax her into demonstrating any of the routines she had learned as a child. "My mother made me drop those lessons for fear that my legs would get too muscled," Mama recalled.

In the early 1940s, Mama had favored a jazz step called Truckin'. I remember coming home from first grade to help start supper. She was perkily shuffling pigeon-toed across the speckled kitchen linoleum, the Philco Transitone atop the dinette table blaring, "Don't Sit Under the Apple Tree." Left hand clutching her midriff, right index finger wagging like a windshield wiper in what she assured me was authentic Truckin' style, she'd nimbly sidestep Suzie, her latest adopted tabby.

She winked at me as she snatched up the potato peeler. I joined her and the Andrew Sisters in the final chorus, "Anyone else but me, no, no, no, anyone else but me," shook my own index finger once or twice, and began to set the table.

The summer before I started high school, Mama taught me the Lindy Hop so that I could go to Town Club dances at the local playground and not be embarrassed. By then I was taking tap and ballet lessons myself, but when it came to pirouettes or pliés, or even a "Shuffle Off to Buffalo" tap maneuver, no amount of pleading could persuade Mama to perform.

Now Mama glanced vacantly around the rec room before bending her head forward to sniff at the crimson carnation corsage pinned to her shoulder. The staff had chosen Mama as Valentine's Day Sweetheart, and I had taken time off work to come to the afternoon party. She wore her favorite, but now-faded, pink-checked gingham dress, and her white hair looked freshly coiffed. Mama had been an ash blond for so many years I'd forgotten it wasn't her original color. I think she had, too.

A tanned, blond male nursing attendant, who looked more suited for a surfboard than a dance floor, switched on the stereo. Tommy Dorsey's sweet trombone swung out on the opening bars of "I'm Getting Sentimental Over You." It had been my parents' favorite. Their eyes always lit up when it came on the radio, and they would leap up and dance around the living room. Mama looked up and smiled. A nurse stepped forward and snapped her photo.

The young man surprised me by gliding toward Mama, proffering his right hand. She moved forward into his arms and they began to float together in an elegant fox-trot, each breaking into grins as applause and cheers erupted from the other residents of the long-term care home. It had been a long time since I had witnessed any signs of mirth cross Mama's face. Other residents began to clamber out of their chairs to join in, snagging partners and tottering toward the floor.

I wondered if Mama would recognize me. The last time I visited, she told the nurses that I was her mother. The time before she thought I was a neighbor. Once or twice she appeared not to know me at all. I just never could tell.

Her partner twirled her out, and Mama double-stepped, not missing a beat, despite the pink satin ballet slippers she wore instead of her customary high-heeled pumps. Mama had always worn high heels, probably because my father was a full foot taller than her barely five feet and one-half-inch frame. That half inch had always been important to her, and she always emphasized it when people asked her height. Even now, years into her bout with Alzheimer's, she still stood erect, though in the past few months she seemed to have dropped ten pounds. Her dress, belted tightly around her tiny waist, flopped loosely around her legs as she danced.

A silver-plaited lady to the right of me, strapped to her wheelchair, began to sing along in a soft but true soprano, petting the tortoiseshell cat curled up in her lap. "Won't you please be kind, and just make up your mind, that you'll be sweet and gentle, gentle with me." I smiled at her and she turned away shyly and fell silent once more.

As the Dorsey number drew to a close, the attendant led Mama toward the vacant seat to my left, but as they neared, she spied the cat and veered toward it. "Suzie," she murmured, "Suzie." The wheelchair-bound woman held up the cat, and Mama snatched it and cuddled it to her bosom. All of her female strays had been Suzies. She called the males Tom. Once there were two male brothers, so she called them Tom and Tom Tom.

She sat beside me, petting the cat. "Mama," I whispered, as the music started up again. This time it was "Little White Lies," and some of the dancers again took the floor. "Mama." I finally reached out my hand and touched her arm. She tore her eyes away from the cat and looked toward me blankly.

One of the nurses headed toward us. "This is your mother, right? She's been practicing her dance steps all week. That's why we decided to make her our Valentine Sweetheart. The others were in favor of it, too." Her hand swept the room. "You know, only three or four residents here have dementia. The others are simply aged. But your mom has been a favorite in the evenings, because she's always willing to get up and dance and to show others how."

I nodded. In the early days even when all the family began to notice that something was not quite right, Mama would still dance. She'd fox-trot with my father in those years before he died. When my brother would visit, he'd teach her country line dances and West Coast swing. One Easter, the entire group of us—me, brothers, parents, aunts, and uncles—all joined in a raucous bunny hop around the living room before heading toward the dining room to feast on Mama's signature tamale pie and cherry fruit salad, one of our last family get-togethers before Father died.

Suddenly Mama turned to me, and then to the nurse. "My sister!" she declared. "This is Terri." I nodded. At least she had my name right. "How are you feeling, Mama?" I asked. But the vacant look had reappeared.

One of the few gentlemen residents walked up. "Luella," he said, "would you care to dance?" Mama jumped to her feet, dumped Suzie into my lap, and clasped her hands in front of her waist. Then she twirled twice and executed a perfect arabesque, which she held for several seconds. A few people clapped, and Mama applauded herself, too, before bowing graciously. She glanced in my direction, and I like to think our eyes caught. The old man laughed, took her hand, and off they glissaded to join the group already swaying to Dorsey. This time it was "Autumn in New York."

Actually, it was winter in Southern California, and I had to get back to work. It had been an eventful afternoon. Mama had remembered my name. It was the last time she ever did. More remarkably, I had finally seen her perform one of those dance moves I'd longed to see throughout my childhood.

Over twenty years later, I still regret not asking the nurse for a copy of that photo. Mama had been my Valentine sweetheart, too—my lost, but sweet, funny Valentine.

♡

Exa

By B. J. Bateman

My seventy-year-old mother, Exa, and I sat rocking on her front porch, thumbing through old photos and talking of her early teaching days.

"In the 1920s my friends were embroidering and leaving fancy calling cards on Sunday afternoons, but I wanted to go to Hawaii," Mother said. "I wanted to see new places, teach school in a new country."

Country? I almost said, then I remembered that Hawaii was still a country in those days.

"But," she continued, "your grandfather felt the whole world was unsafe because of the recently ended world war, and he refused to let me go." She smiled and said, "I just didn't want to put on an apron and take my expected place in the kitchen."

"So instead you campaigned for Granddaddy for Congress."

"Yes. In fact, it's rumored that I was the first woman in the United States to campaign for a man for public office, but you never know about statistics."

"Mother, that's still incredible."

"Not so much," she said, smiling again. "He didn't win." We laughed and sipped our iced tea in the muggy East Texas heat.

She didn't set out to be different; Mother just blazed her own path at a time when female path blazing was not a common practice. That path began in the piney woods of East Texas. She was the product of a "proper" family. Her father, an attorney, never came to the dinner table without coat and tie. In front of others he referred to his wife as Mrs. Beavers, never Betty. Perhaps it was against this staid upbringing that Mother, in her own way, rebelled.

Besides the albums, her college yearbook lay on a table between us. On one page I saw she'd studied Latin and French, played tennis, and graduated with honors. On another my mother sported regulation black pantaloons and a white middy blouse, while holding a basketball under one arm.

"Mother, you played basketball?"

"Oh, yes, and I even coached a girls' team for a while. You didn't know the old girl had it in her, did you?"

I didn't and was amazed.

I opened one of the albums and discovered a picture of a little hardware store facing a rutted dirt road. Through the open door one could see barrels, coils of rope, and what looked like oil rigging supplies.

"That was in the 1930s," Mother offered. "The world was riding the rails and grocery shopping in garbage cans. Your dad heard about an oil discovery out in the panhandle and nothing would do but for us to pick up and go seek our fortune. So we ended up with a little hardware store on the West Texas prairie. And, get this, I even ran for city commissioner while helping your father in that struggling hardware store."

The next sepia print was of Mother holding me, a newborn, to her breast. On the opposite page was a picture of a flower-bedecked grave, that of my two-year-old brother who had died of an ear infection when I was just four months old. No penicillin in those days. She ran her fingertips across the picture. "That little Jimmy was quite a boy. Did you know we could give him a dime to walk down the block to the drugstore for ice cream and he knew whether to wait for change or not?" She smiled, straightened her shoulders, and flipped the page.

"We were short of schoolteachers in West Texas," she said. "So I wrote letters to your aunt Lula and cousin Hallieah and told them to come on out." My aunt Lula was Mother's youngest sibling. As the baby, she had spent her childhood days roaming up and down Beavers Street visiting all the neighbors. Aunt Lula's full name was Lula Mildred Beavers, but at each neighborhood household, she added their name to hers, thus she used to recite her name as Lula Mildred Beavers Stein Thomas Daily and so on for a total of eleven names. When she grew older she would tell my mother that the more parents loved their children, the more names they were given. Since Exa Beavers were the only two names Mother had, Lula thought that told the story.

I continued thumbing through the pages and stopped at a picture of two young black women. "These are Missy's two girls whose college tuition you paid, right? Weren't their names Pat and Joann?"

"Yes. Pat and Jo were sweet girls, and Missy was a very special woman."

At a time when segregation was an accepted practice and women's lib an unknown term, Mother quietly financed the college education of Pat and Jo while their mother did our washing and ironing. Missy was more than a washwoman, however. Hanging on a wall in my home is an old quilt top, spattered with colorful cotton butterflies pieced by Missy.

But while Missy's girls were still in school, the cry went up, rallying our nation to another war. My father had hopped a train to Oregon in pursuit of war work. Some weeks later, Mother stored our furniture with relatives and packed for what everyone assumed would be a six-month war. "We're joining your daddy in a wartime city called Vanport out in Oregon. He's got a job building ships for the war."

After three days and nights on a coal-burning train, we arrived in Portland to find that our sooty appearance fit right in with the seedy hotel in which my dad had reserved the only room he could find for the three of us. We shared a bath down the hall with defense workers and our sheets with bedbugs. Lodging was scarce.

Our first glimpse of Vanport was on move-in day a month later. The new city was a confusing place of identical gray apartment buildings nestled in a sea of mud. It soon became a quagmire of twenty-four-hour shifts, clanking lunch pails, air-raid drills, and service uniforms. Such challenge and chaos was Exa's cup of tea. That first Christmas, she hauled a Christmas tree home on the bus because she knew it would be important to me. My father and I enjoyed a stewed chicken Christmas dinner that Mother prepared on a two-burner stove. Soon she set about to help found a

Methodist church in a junior high school building and took a job with the housing authority.

After the war, she and my father separated, and eventually, after I'd graduated from high school, she returned to Texas. There, in the 1960s, when the young were protesting and saying the system had nothing to offer but turmoil, Mother didn't notice. She was managing an insurance agency, teaching church school on Sundays, and sending five-dollar bills wrapped in letters of encouragement to my husband and me.

"Thought you might be able to buy the babies a toy or something," her note would say. She probably knew we would buy a loaf of bread or a bottle of milk. It was several years later that I told her just how important those enclosures were. Once, two one-dollar bills tucked within a letter allowed us to pay the paperboy and even give him a small tip. Another tuck-in came just in time for us to get a prescription filled for cough syrup desperately needed for our sick little girl.

In the 1970s, at a time when the "me generation" was accumulating, protecting, and climbing corporate ladders, my mother was holding down her job at the insurance office by day and cooking and delivering the evening meal to her brother, who was suffering from emphysema, by night. She'd stay to tidy his apartment before returning to her own home. Sundays, after church, she relaxed by playing pinochle with friends.

Mother and I had spent a lot of time together over books through the years. From the time I was very young, each afternoon she read with me. Dick, Jane, Spot, and I became such good friends that before I entered school, I could read the first grade primer all the way through. Thanks to Mother, I still have a love affair with books.

As a senior in high school I was among the finalists for Rose Festival princess from our school. Each day, following interviews and other rigors, the surviving competitors' names were posted. And each night, for as long as my name stayed on the list, Mother sat down at her sewing machine and made me a new skirt, blouse, or dress to wear for the next day's test. Once I had the new outfit on, she'd step back to admire, adjust a shoulder, give me a hug, and say, "Give 'em your best."

Mother gave life her best. She majored in literature, played college sports, engaged in public affairs, ignored segregation practices, ran for office, and picked up and moved during wartime. All the while she was a caring, loving mother. My mother, Exa, was an amazing nurturer and adventurer, a woman who lived ahead of her time. I'd give her more than eleven names.

♡

The Pink Slippers

By Roberta McGovern

The last gift my mother gave me before she died was a pair of ugly pink slippers. Ever practical, she knew that while not pretty, they would keep my feet warm and probably last forever. They *were* warm and they *did* seem to last forever. They got dirty and faded but still kept my feet warm.

We moved several times, and each time we moved I thought, *I really should get rid of these things*, because by now they were frayed, worn, and almost colorless, but they still kept my feet warm. They were familiar, like an old friend, and I always felt comfortable when I put them on.

My daughter, who was helping me pack for our move to Florida, not understanding my attachment to these ugly, "holey" things, threw them away, but I retrieved them from the trash can and they made the trip to Florida with us.

I rarely wore them because they were so ratty, and they were stashed away in the back of the closet, but occasionally something would remind me that they were there and I could always stick my feet in them, wiggle my toes, and feel warm and comfortable.

Finally, the day came when there were more holes than slippers and I knew that it was time to throw them away. It was sad though, like losing an old, familiar friend. I then realized that the slippers had become a symbol of my mother's love for me, her desire to keep me warm, safe, and secure, no matter what. These slippers, like my mother, had comforted me through a lot of tough times. I could always turn to them in a time of need, stick my feet in, wiggle my toes, and find comfort, and they were always there—hidden away, old, and tired, but still there.

But, just as my mother had died, I knew there was a time for all things, and it was time to let those slippers go. However, among my little box of memories, along with locks of my children's hair and the menu from the restaurant where my husband and I ate on our first date is a small scrap of ugly, frayed, dirty pink fabric from the sole of my mother's final gift to me, reminding me of her love and care, which will always be with me.

♡

Newspapers and Snowballs

By John J. Lesjack

"Newspapers!" shouted my mother, looking out the frosty kitchen window. "Dress warm!"

Despite the blizzard that raged throughout Michigan that Saturday afternoon, my bundle of newspapers was delivered right on time. Dinosaur-size snowdrifts formed around most buildings in our neighborhood. Dad had left early and crunched his way to the corner where a bus soon swallowed him up and took him to his factory job. This cold January day found my siblings plopped down inside the East Detroit Theater watching cowboy movies. Mom had fed them an early lunch and then dropped them off around noon. My newspaper route waited for me, so I bundled up in heavy winter clothes.

Mom looked at the living room, empty of children, and returned to her kitchen. She sprinkled crackers on a pot of macaroni and cheese, slid it into the oven, set the temperature, and closed the oven door. "Johnny, you can't go out in that storm alone. I'll drive you," she said as she pulled off her apron.

Apparently, there was no limit to the changes the weather would cause that day. I packed my newspapers in the front seat, Mom backed out of the driveway, and we headed down the road. Just as I realized I was alone with Mom, she began laughing. "There's your grandpa's overalls," she said. She pointed to frozen laundry on a neighbor's clothesline. "They'd make a good scarecrow."

Mom drove slowly as the wind nudged the car and swirls of snow reduced visibility. She had no chains on the tires. We agreed that I would deliver at least six newspapers with each stop. I soon got out of the car, stepped into a pile of snow that came up to my knees, and trudged up to each house. In 1948, I put the newspaper inside the storm door.

After deliveries on our street were completed, we turned a corner, traveled west, and crossed some railroad tracks. During this nonstop part of the route, Mom told me about her childhood on a farm in Canada.

"During weather like this, my dad tied a rope onto our house and ran it out to the barn. He held on to the rope when he went out to the barn to feed the animals. That way, he didn't get lost."

She shifted into second gear for the first time that day and continued, "When the snow was piled twelve or fifteen feet high, my dad followed that rope and dug a tunnel out to the barn. I used the tunnel when I had to go out and feed the chickens. In the evening, my dad would bring a washtub full of clean snow into the kitchen. My mother would heat up maple syrup to make taffy. She'd pour the syrup onto the snow," Mom said. " I loved taffy-in-the-snow."

Our old car climbed over the railroad tracks easily, but Mom lost control coming down, and we slid into a ditch where the back wheels spun uselessly. We looked at each other. All Mom said was, "Uh-oh."

I trudged to my closest stop, a farmhouse, and knocked on the door.

The farmer's tractor pulled us out, but as we left the ditch, the car began sliding back and forth, and Mom got silly. "Whee!" she said, as the car slid to the right. "Whoa!" she laughed as it slid to the left. Then it hit a bump, and we both laughed like schoolkids on a ride at the fairgrounds. Mom was usually very serious. Laughing with her was a memorable and enjoyable treat. Somehow, she made it fun to get stuck in a ditch. When I looked over at my mother, her cheeks were rosy from the cold air, and I was embarrassed to think that she was actually pretty.

After my last delivery, the wind had stopped, briefly. But as I walked toward the car, a snowball went flying past my head. What the—? I looked up just as another snowball hit me in the chest. I saw my mother laughing and throwing snowballs! She gave me no choice. Soon, we could barely distinguish snowballs from snow flurries flying through the air. She threw like a girl, but what a thrill it was to play in the snow with my mother. I wished she would always be this much fun.

Suddenly, she yelled, "Let's go home! I left the oven on!" We giggled all the way home.

Mom set the macaroni on the stove and then went down into the basement. She shoveled coal into the furnace and banked the fire. She checked the laundry drying on the lines down there. Later, she drove to the bus stop to get Dad, then into town because the movies were letting out.

Six children and two adults put their feet under the same table that night and enjoyed dinner together. Mom said grace. It was good to have a stay-at-home mom.

Forty winters after 1948, the year of that great snowstorm and the year my dad died, my daughter and I were in the mountains on a ski trip. As I parked the car in an area dug out by a snow-plow, I said, "This reminds me of the time my mother drove me around my paper route during a snowstorm." Mom and I had never talked about that fun time. Or maybe we had, and I was unwilling to remember a happy feeling so soon after my father's death. Who knows?

Years later, during my daughter's wedding events, after my two remaining sisters and I were caught up on children and grand-children news, we began reminiscing about our mother. One sis-ter recalled that Mom had driven my sister and her date to a junior high dance. My other sister mentioned that weeds had replaced flowers around Mom's old house. The tenant was not keeping up the place.

Head down, I cleared my throat and said, "Did you ever hear about the time Mom drove me around my paper route and we ended up throwing snowballs at each other?" When I looked up, my sisters were smiling, so I said, "Mom was a lot of fun that day."

♡

Our Child

By Kathe Campbell

She was my darlin', a no-bigger-than-a-minute, beautiful, smart mom who retired from an accounting career after Dad left her a young widow. She maintained a lovely condo, loved her children's charities, and enjoyed a busy social life. I was Gran's only adopted child; we were close, and she looked forward to holidays in our mountain home.

During a late summer Granny visit in the 1970s, my family noted things going awry. Neither Gran's earrings nor her shoes matched, and she was oddly flustered. She agonized over preparing a simple meal, all of us noting refrigerated items in various growing stages. Always the most fastidious woman and good cook, her once-impeccable surroundings had become unkempt.

Her checkbook seemed her mortal enemy as she persisted in public exhibitions in her bank lobby. "Mr. Big Shot," she addressed the tellers pompously, "you have walked off with all my money. You are inefficient and I intend to prosecute!" Gratefully, her dear neighbor rescued Gran from the aggravation and balanced her checks for her.

The short months of baffling personality changes had left me dumbfounded. I had heard of Alzheimer's disease but had no clue what was happening in those early stages. Scarcely any physician could, or would, diagnose the disease, nor were there any drugs to impede its onset. Gran's doctors said she was experiencing extreme dementia, never once mentioning the word Alzheimer's. Because she was continually becoming lost and a danger to pedestrians, friends took over as chauffeurs for Gran's appointments.

In early fall, our daughter, Molly, and I journeyed to the coast on the pretext of having Gran spend her holidays in Montana. She was playing cards, so we waited until the elevator doors slid open and Gran sailed down the hall with fire in her eyes. "Who are you, anyway?" she demanded. I could see tears welling in Molly's eyes, but she quickly rebounded, "It's us, Gran—Mom and Molly," whereupon I kissed her cheek and told her we were going out for dinner. With a loathsome glare, she shoved her purse under her mattress, slammed the bedroom door, and grumbled about us being the last thing she needed. We stood stunned.

That evening Molly and I helped a reluctant Gran dress for dinner. At the dimly lit restaurant, Molly ordered wine. Gran became giddy, talking and laughing loudly. People stared and smiled politely, but it felt wonderful seeing her cheerful and affectionate. We had our Gran on a toot, and she was having a ball; that's all that mattered.

The holidays in our home seemed a much happier and relaxed time for Gran. She adored the kitty and dog, petting them endlessly. I kept a supply of cookies on hand for afternoon tea and the chats where I learned to simply agree with her every word.

She soon forgot her condo, old friends, and her sweet neighbor. I was met daily by her quizzical Irish eyes beneath dark curls swathed in wings of white as she reached for my hand to ask, "Who are you?"

Gran and I went shopping, to lunch, and the hairdresser's weekly. Making me her hero and allaying her constant money worries, I introduced Gran to our bank president. Our doctor educated us on her small stroke showers, how to handle them, and encouraged continued loving care with no confrontations. *Oh Lordy*, I pondered. He obviously knew little about living with Alzheimer's, for every week saw my darlin' sinking into yet another unfamiliar abyss.

While I had a tendency to lose it, my husband, Ken, was an angel with Gran as her hell-roaring years passed. He fixed her lovely breakfasts, my evening meals audibly christened with her uncharacteristic curses. She minded him and he respected her as the matriarch of our family, even though the matriarch was fast becoming a vestige of her former self. At long last Ken became the "Mr." and I was "that lady!"

So Ken and I bit the bullet, for my mother was now our child, and despite moments of near defeat, we kept one step ahead of every phase. Our other daughter, KT, periodically came home from college with a friend or two. "You and Dad should get out of the house for dinner and a movie, Mom. I'm good at handling things, so go and don't worry."

Thus, KT and company weathered Gran's first flirt with disaster. She had donned shoes and slipped outdoors into the blackness of trees whipping wildly in a rainstorm. The girls were frantic until finding her in the barn, naked as a jaybird, patting and comforting four unruffled horses. "Poor things were frightened to death, dear," Gran argued unashamedly. We discovered her shredded nightie in tall pine limbs, like pink banners waving first light greetings to the new day. Knowing my mom, she would have laughed hysterically over such an incident.

Bizarre nurturing evolved, characterized by chaos and disorder, the latter months a whole different ball game. I was dealing with eighty pounds of hellcat whose mind had turned to Jell-O, though I could recognize the soul and spirit of a champion beneath. She spoke well when belligerent, stood and walked with a wobble, and thrust daggers of hate. I must have told the grandchildren a thousand times that it wasn't Gran under there. She was divested of her sweet smile and laughter, personality, memories, love of family, and worst of all, her dignity. That seemed like no quality of life at all.

I sometimes lay those five years to rest, but I occasionally find myself recalling and, yes, laughing about them as my toughest crusade. I dare not even imagine what it would've been like without levity and strong family support. I have no regrets, and I would gladly do it again, for Alzheimer's itself is the degrading horror story, not our dear ones who suffer from it.

Sometimes I hear her sweet, soft voice . . . "Dearest daughter, the scrapbook of my entire life faded into useless mist—thank you for setting me free!"

Teddy Bear, Ready to Go

By Marilyn A. Gelman

My mother's acquaintance, Paula, was a librarian who traveled with tour groups on every vacation. She kept a list of places she wanted to revisit after retirement. My mother was bitten by the travel bug but always stayed close to home. Although Dad would go to Catskills resorts with his lodge brothers and their wives, he considered that he had paid his travel dues while courting Mom in Brooklyn from his home in New Jersey.

As their friends traveled to hot spots abroad, Mom was anguished, but Dad was adamant. When he finally did take flight, he loved it, but, sadly, he died soon after his maiden voyage.

One day, my mom and her friend Paula got to talking, and, beginning a tradition, Mom summoned me to her apartment for a serious discussion. She reminded me of how she longed to see the world outside of New Jersey, told me about Paula's list of favorite places. She said Paula was going to China and wanted her to go, too. Mom could not afford to travel on her small salary as a part-time secretary to the rabbi of the biggest temple in town. She would have to use some of my "portion."

My "portion" was the sum of money my mother expected to leave me when she died. She was not a wealthy woman, but she had stashed a little of Dad's insurance money in certificates of deposit to leave for my brother and me. The "portion" was something greater than its dollar value.

I said, "Be sure you use my entire portion first. I want you to have fun on my piece of it." This was brave talk from a single parent who worried about paying the electric bill, but I meant it.

In those days, China was just opening up to tourism. My mother was not the best candidate for an extraordinary travel experience. She was a senior citizen, and she was legally blind; a childhood disease had taken her night vision and most of her peripheral vision, too. She needed an arm to lean on for guidance in unfamiliar territory in daylight; she needed a strong arm to help her in the dark.

Paula knew what she was getting into, my portion was set, and the trip was on. The night before Mom left, my sons and I visited to bid her bon voyage and sneak a little going-away present into her luggage—a small teddy bear.

That gift would give my mother quite a scare. Unpacking in her hotel at night, with only a dim, bare bulb illuminating the room, she reached into her suitcase and felt something furry. Without knowing what bugs or little animals inhabited China, she needed courage to keep her hand on the object and pull it out. Mom was embarrassed, afraid Paula would think she packed the comfort toy herself.

At the group's first dinner in China, the guide said they and their possessions would always be safe in his country. He reassured them when gunshots rang out. Stray dogs had been rounded up, he said, and were being shot in the square. This was to make China safer for its visitors.

But I read the newspapers while my mom was in China. Petty thieves and pickpockets had been rounded up and shot in the square to make China safe for tourists. And during her trip, China threatened to stop foreign tourism. I didn't care if they let no one else in as long as they let my mother's group out.

When Mom described the Great Wall of China, I thought back a few years to her complaint about the great hill she climbed every workday in Paterson, New Jersey. Shortly after Dad had died, Mom's vision had changed. The eye doctor said she was going blind, but she told no one. When her doctor died, her new doctor refuted the prognosis but couldn't understand why her cataracts had not been removed. After the procedure, Mom complained about her walk to work. She had regularly climbed one of the steepest hills in town without recognizing the sharpness of the incline. She could only see one step ahead and she took that step, then the next, then the next. But with Paula, Mom would climb many walls and use pit toilets in dark caves.

A great traveling team had been born! I was summoned to Mom's apartment many times for my "portion" conferences. My answer was always the same. The teddy bear went to Yugoslavia, Greece, Switzerland, London, and Israel. Mom thought the world was a big place, but my sons and I would telephone her once each trip to let her know she couldn't get away from us, no matter where she went.

Once, the women ran into trouble. In Switzerland, Paula

bought a huge chef's knife and packed it in her purse for safe-keeping on their trip home. They were marching single file through airport security, Mom's hand clutching Paula's shoulder, when alarms shrieked; Paula was whisked away. Mom stood frozen until an official came to her aid. But as she went through security, more alarms sounded. Mom was hustled to a little room where, she said, she was touched in places no one had touched her since my father had died. Paula promised the authorities she would pack all big knives in checked luggage in the future. My mother thought it was all hilarious.

Although I worried about group safety in China, I worried about Mom's personal safety as she prepared for their London trip. She and Paula were to sail over on the Queen Elizabeth II and spend ten days going to shows and shopping. They rented a little place where they could prepare light suppers and spend the evenings playing gin rummy. But we had noticed that Mom's hearing had taken a turn for the worse and lobbied diligently for her to go to the hearing aid place.

Mom and the hearing aid lady knew each other from Paterson organizations. When I took her to the appointment, I looked for professional support.

"I told my mother," I said, "that I was worried. She can't see oncoming traffic out of the corners of her eyes; cars come from a different direction over there, and if she can't hear either. . . ."

"Not to worry," my mother assured us. "Paula and I have it all worked out. I can't hear in one ear, and she can't hear in one ear. We hold on to each other so that each of us has a good ear pointed in a different direction. We hear everything."

The hearing aid lady looked at me to see if I laughed. I didn't. She told my mom, "It doesn't work that way." Major changes were needed to Mom's hearing aid, but they were completed before her trip.

During her final illness, Mom still had the travel bug. She was to go to Florida, meet up with relatives, and take a cruise. She asked the doctor's opinion.

"Go," he said. "If you need an IV, the doctor on board can hook you up; they're equipped. You can drip on a ship just as well as you can drip in the hospital. And the food's probably better. Go."

I was summoned for a last serious discussion about my portion and a shopping foray for something snazzy to wear, but my mother did not get to make that last trip. When she died, a bright yellow designer-label ensemble—a jacket, Bermuda shorts, and a mini-skirt bought at discount—was hanging in her closet near a big battered suitcase on wheels inside of which was a little teddy bear ready to go.

Late in life, of modest means, widowed, with no worldly travel experience, legally blind, and partially deaf, my mother had seen more of the world than New Jersey.

Bon voyage, Mom. *L'chaim* (to life)!

Final Words

By Wayne Scheer

You know that old Gertrude Stein and Alice B. Toklas anecdote where Alice asks Gertrude on her deathbed, "What is the answer?" and Gertrude responds, "What is the question?"

Most of us don't die with such grace, with our final words offering a profound memorial to our lives. My mother lived with my wife and me during the end of her life. She suffered from congenital heart failure, dragging her oxygen machine from room to room like an unwilling dance partner. The night she died, she mustered what strength she had to leave me a parting note: "Wayne. There's a bad odor coming from the bathroom sink. Fix it."

Not exactly words to commemorate a life.

But dying words aren't the way to remember a life. Death is rarely about dignity. That's what life is for.

My mother lived a life of honor, remaining true to her own unique code. Some might call her adherence to her way small-minded and her belief that everyone else should follow controlling —I know I did—but I came to realize that her demands were her expression of love.

A tad over five feet and barely one hundred pounds in her prime, she had a steadiness that suggested sturdiness. My father's nickname for her was "Little Napoleon," which he used endearingly. She ruled the family, as well as our extended family.

She had her own way of expressing her demands. I remember hearing her on the telephone berating her brother for not calling. "Telephones are two-way streets," she scolded, without a trace of humor.

She had a Yogi Berra–like take on language, once advising me to "take the bull by the horns and run with it." After attending a religious service, she said, "I'd go more often if it wasn't for all that God stuff."

My dry sense of humor obviously came from my mother. To this day, I don't know how much of what she said was intentional and how much just slipped out of her mouth, as if the censor most of us have in our heads had malfunctioned. When she lived with us, she watched my wife clean the kitchen. Barely able to stand on her own, she still managed a zinger. "Your mother wasn't much of a housekeeper, was she?" she asked.

Fortunately, by that time, my wife had grown to both love and tolerate my mother (an essential combination), so she just smiled and held her tongue.

My wife's relationship with my mom really began when I was drafted during the Vietnam War. Just two years into our marriage, we were living two thousand miles from home when the army decided it wanted me. My wife tried keeping a semblance of the life we had been building, but she needed an anchor and came to depend upon my mother's Sunday morning phone call as well as her long, rambling letters, which arrived like clockwork every other day.

I remember those letters. Long before cell phones and free minutes, my mother wrote. She wrote me when I went to college, and she wrote when I was in the army. Ten to twelve pages of unlined paper wasn't unusual as she filled me in on the minutia of family—what she cooked that day, who in the family had a cold, the high school grades of a cousin. Later, I discovered she sheltered me from the harsh side of family gossip. She never shared the juicy stories I'd learn from my sister about who was divorcing or sleeping with whom. It always amazed me how her supposed malfunctioning censor could work so well to protect me from the seamy side of life.

It was her way of showing her love for me, her firstborn, and this angered my sister to no end. My mother came from another era, where women ruled the home and not the workplace. In her mind, she prepared me to support a family, while she trained my sister to run it. I don't know if my sister ever truly understood that distinction.

From as early as I could remember, she made it clear I was going to be the first male in our family to go to college. At the beginning of kindergarten, I remember her counting with me: "eight years of grammar school, four years of high school, and four years of college." I had no choice.

She had always been a stay-at-home mom, which was not unusual in the fifties. But somewhere around the time I entered high school, she took a job in a local department store. She told me she needed to get out of the house now that my sister and I were older. My father also began working overtime, something he had avoided the way others stayed clear of a sneezing child. It took me years to realize they were saving money to send me to college.

My mother, a woman who never went beyond the eighth grade, had a profound respect for education. She understood it would be my way to a better life long before I did. When I lacked the motivation to study, she pushed and prodded. She hired a tutor when I had problems with high school algebra, never allowing me to even consider the expense.

The cost of college never appeared to be an issue, although their lifestyle was decidedly Spartan. My mother behaved as though it were sinful to spend money on herself, while my father simply didn't believe in spending money. Still, when it came time for me to attend college, the money appeared as if by magic. I discovered by accident that they had taken out a bank loan to pay my tuition for my junior and senior years. They refused to talk about it. My mother simply said, "That's our business."

One of my proudest moments occurred years later when my wife and I presented my parents with a check covering the approximate cost of my college tuition. My mother wept. My father talked of them traveling. But true to form, they eventually used the money to buy a car for my sister who had recently divorced.

My mother was as prolific as Thomas Wolfe when it came to chronicling family life—and as ferocious as a she-wolf when it came to protecting it. As much as I rebelled against her demanding and controlling ways, I've come to admire her sense of family responsibility. Even after she died, my sister and I discovered letters from her in a safe-deposit box, demanding that we remain close and threatening to haunt us if we didn't. "Pick up a phone," she wrote me. "It won't kill you." She wrote the same words to my sister, adding, "It's up to you to keep in touch with your cousins. And make sure Wayne does, too." To her grandchildren, she wrote, "Stay close, work hard in school, and be good citizens."

Maybe her final words were worthy of commemoration after all.

♡

Life in a Box

By Nancy Viau

Anniversary. . . .

Prior to this year, I used this word to describe a joyous celebration. It was connected with life, not death.

The anniversary of my mother's death weighed on my mind and disrupted all thought processes for an entire week. One year had passed, and I still couldn't erase the vision of her in the hospital bed. I hoped to seek some closure, so I ventured to the basement where Mom's treasures were stored. I needed to find something that would help me reflect upon her life, not dwell on her death.

I started down the steps and went through the sequence of events that put me in this state of mind. My parents lived miles away, so Mom and I often exchanged letters. She wrote about recipes, new books, and day-to-day events. One letter had a postscript: "I'm having trouble with my back, but I'm handling it."

I learned that doctors attributed her discomfort to fractures in the spine due to osteoporosis. Medicines were prescribed. Time passed. Soon Mom became so consumed with pain she was unable to leave the couch. She was admitted to the hospital, and

I caught the next plane. By the time I arrived, the specialists had already made their diagnosis. They spoke the words I feared— lung cancer, throughout the chest and back. And it was terminal.

Dad dried the endless tears that streamed down my cheeks. "This should not be a surprise," he said, holding his emotions in check.

No truer words were spoken. Mom had been a smoker for almost sixty years.

As I went to her side, she stated without fanfare, "It doesn't look good."

I pushed down the anger swelling inside me. I wanted to scream at her for every cigarette that she had inhaled that added to the blackness in her lungs and the gray mass evident in her body, but words were useless now.

Instead, we simply hugged, and she asked, "How are the kids?"

As was Mom's style, she did not complain or feel compelled to discuss her diagnosis. She understood the truth and accepted it. And she wanted me to do the same.

During the following week, Mom needed more and more painkillers. Morphine pumped into her veins, and she eventually lapsed into a semi-comatose state. Each new day I discovered deeper creases puncturing her face—evidence of pain not quieted by powerful drugs.

I longed to see the sparkle in her green eyes and hear her cheery voice. She remained motionless as I read cards, sang favorite songs, and held her—never wanting to let go. "You are the best mom anyone could have asked for," I whispered. "Stay with me a little longer."

But three days later, she died.

In the months to come, Dad sorted through Mom's personal belongings. He thoughtfully placed clothes, jewelry, and more into categories: "Give Away," "Sell," "Save." And he moved in with me.

I did get to the bottom of the basement stairs that day, and I discovered what I needed—the box that contained items from the "Save" category. I lifted the lid and was overcome by Mom's scent. She seemed to be with me as I went through what was there: school yearbooks, graduation and wedding photographs, newspaper articles, war memorabilia, journals, and, of course, letters decades old from siblings and friends, children and grandchildren.

I sat for hours among delightful fragments of my mother's life and discovered so much more than items in a box. I got to know her as a skinny preteen dressed in ankle socks and loafers; a high school basketball star; a poised young woman who stole boys' hearts; a war correspondent; a devoted sister, friend, and newlywed; and finally as a mother who was especially at ease when photographed with a baby snuggled in her arms.

I realized that while she was alive, I unintentionally viewed her only as Mom or Grandmom. I was selfishly unconcerned with what occurred before my birth.

But what I found in that box on that anniversary day was what was significant in *one woman's life*—before and after my arrival. It was *her entire life*—and it was depicted in items that lingered in a simple cardboard cubicle.

I am grateful for those tangible items that cleared my mind and helped me through a sad time. Visions of Mom on her deathbed no longer haunt me. I take comfort in remembering her, not only as Mother, who trimmed my bangs, sewed my prom dresses, and cried at my wedding, but also as a truly amazing individual who shared a portion of her life with me.

One day in the future, someone will sort through my belongings. I wonder what items will be chosen that speak of my days here on Earth. . . .

What will end up in my box?

♡

Mom's Gelatin

By Todd Outcalt

Even the best of mothers sometimes bear the brunt of their children's teasing—some of it even mean-spirited or misdirected. During the years my brother and I were at home, we often made fun of our mother's cooking.

Mom, in her frugality, loved to serve up mounds of gelatin dotted with marshmallows or pineapple chunks. There were also recipes featuring lime gelatin mixed with applesauce and raspberry gelatin sprinkled with shaved coconut—and not always in small portions.

Mom's gelatin molds were frequently unsheathed from Bundt cake tins, and, when the occasion necessitated, from mammoth turkey pans that could feed an army. No doubt, every bone in our house was strong, and my brother and I secretly suspected that our mother served up so much gelatin because she feared we might die of the rickets.

Mom also saved money by cooking up the likes of tuna pizza (made of Bisquick batter), celery sticks covered with cream cheese, and fried potatoes lathered in generic ketchup. And how could we forget the stuffed peppers and pickle loaf served on white bread?

Mom always endured our ribbing about her cooking with a smile.

Of course, as children grow older, they can look back and explore the nuances of their parents' lives. They begin to see how well their parents did, given the circumstances, and why some of the discussions, events, and, yes, even meals, were momentous occasions.

Now we can see that Mom's cooking was a show of strength. It had to be. After all, Mom was a public school teacher for forty-two years, and most of her days didn't end at the dinner table. There were papers to grade, lesson plans to create, phone calls to make, and scores to record—all of this in addition to keeping up with the household chores, being a leader at church, and attending a myriad of sporting events. Streamlined cooking was Mom's way of making the most of the time and giving us everything we needed. It wasn't just our bones she kept strong, but our spirits as well.

Despite Mom's many commitments and responsibilities, she was always present. I can't think of a single instance when she wasn't there for us. And even when she was sick, she often took care of the rest of the family.

Unlike most of my friends, I don't have many memories of my mother in the kitchen. Rather, I remember a mom who always drove me to the next baseball or basketball game, sat next to me in church, helped me with my homework, cheered for me in the stands, and gave me advice when it was time to go to college. Mom didn't pass along any recipes, but she did pass along plenty of insights, good values, and, most of all, her friendship.

It's been years since I've eaten from a gelatin mold the size of a washtub, but I can't even eat a bowl of gelatin without thinking of Mom or calling her on the phone. And sometimes, if the gelatin is lime-flavored, I even make a meal of it.

But I really miss the marshmallows.

Must-Know Info

MUST-KNOW INFO

Finding Your Unique Parenting Style

Leslie Godwin, author, From Burned Out to Fired Up

Y ou've read the books, listened to your mom, fended off your in-laws, and gotten advice from your girlfriends, pediatrician, and hairdresser. Now it's time to tune in to your intuition and discover your unique parenting style.

This process is a lot like figuring out your career path, or what a good marriage means to you. You take in a variety of helpful advice, tips, and examples from mentors and parents, and after you've looked outside for answers, it's time to look within to your inner wisdom for guidance.

Here are some tips to help you make this a more conscious process:

1. **Set your sights on the big picture.** Think about what you most hope your child's values and character will be when they're fifteen, twenty-five, and forty-five years old. What does this look like? How can you model those values now?

I've done a lot of coaching with entrepreneurs to grow their businesses while putting their families first. One consistent challenge is developing the ability to switch back and forth between the big picture and day-to-day tasks. Without the big picture, they can't lead others or guide their business. And, of course, if they don't pay the bills, clean the office, and return phone calls, they have no business to grow.

It's hard to balance getting through each day—making meals and snacks, chauffeuring our children to and from activities, and doing loads of laundry—with shepherding our children from helpless infancy to becoming responsible, decent, and caring adults.

I believe the secret to both of these challenges is to start with the big picture. Then spell out what that looks like in your day-to-day life. Break your goals down and include them in your weekly and daily calendar to-do lists. Then fit in the rest of your chores and activities.

2. **Pick your battles.** While pulling her whining three-year-old son off her leg, a friend recently asked me what is the single best parenting tip I could give anyone struggling with their young child. "Pick your battles" instantly came to mind. I think there are several reasons for this being at the top of my list:

- We don't have enough energy to fight every battle.
- Our kids tune out so quickly that strategic strikes work best. ("When you are rough with the dog, she'll be rough, too. Let's try petting her gently.") And boys tune out twice as fast as girls, so you do well to speak in a telegraphic style. ("Stop! Pet her gently.")
- When you don't focus your energy on the issues you care

about most, you water down your limited parenting power.

• If you try to address too many issues, you'll probably be spending a lot of time nagging, reminding, and—let's be honest—annoying your child. If you want your home to be your child's and spouse's safe haven, pick one or two battles and call it a day.

I've found it helpful to write down what I most care about when it comes to parenting my three-year-old son. Character was clearly the big-ticket item. So I do my best to keep my nagging in perspective. If he's (basically) a good guy, (usually) only "fights" bad guys, is kind to animals, and (mostly) respectful to adults, I'm doing my job. If his room is messy and he hasn't learned three words that start with the letter "C" yet, I'm not going to stress out.

3. **Use your intuition.** Like the cartoon character with an angel on one shoulder and a devil on the other, we each host an inner battle between opposing voices. One is our inner critic. That's the one that tells you that you really should fit into your skinny jeans by now. Or that you'll never be an artist, so don't bother signing up for the painting workshop you've dreamed about taking.

Our positive inner voice is our intuition. That's the calm, wise voice we hear when we know it's time to take a deep breath before we yell at our child. It also lets us know that it must be naptime or snacktime before our child knows he's sleepy or hungry. Mother's intuition doesn't kick in right away. I was a parenting "expert" for thirteen years before I had my first child, and it still took me over a year as a new mom to be able to count on it. But we can develop our intuition and learn to ignore our inner critic.

Each time you tune in to your intuition, you're reinforcing it. After you do this over and over again, your intuition will get stronger and you'll gain confidence in it.

4. Take a break when you've reached the breaking point. You can't use your intuition when you're anxious or your baby is crying (I know that is redundant). If you have a hard time pulling yourself away when you're getting into a power struggle, and most of us do, form the habit by asking a trusted friend to let you know when you need to take a breather.

Once you get used to doing this, both you and your child will anticipate when it's time to settle yourself down. By the way, this is the best strategy to teach your child to use a time-out to settle themselves down. I don't always succeed, but I try not to make a time-out a punishment. It's a consequence, but it's also a method our children can use to calm themselves.

The bonus round of this technique is to build in breaks before you reach your breaking point. This isn't natural, and it's not always attainable, but if you have a laser focus on taking care of yourself so you can be the mom your child needs, more often than not you can find a way to get a half hour break, take a shower, or even squeeze in a nap. I used to feel guilty when my husband watched my son so I could get a nap. (This was my inner critic at work.) But once I realized that my husband preferred interrupting his workday to having a cranky wife, I let go of the guilt, and when I need to nap and he's home, I can count on him helping me out.

5. **Pray, practice your faith, and ask for guidance if you are spiritual.** Don't you try to ask the most qualified source possible for whatever has you puzzled or overwhelmed? Sometimes that's a pediatrician, sometimes your spouse, but often it's God. Not everyone identifies with asking God for parenting advice, and I absolutely respect that. But if you are spiritual, think about when it's best to ask your Higher Power for guidance. If you're not spiritual, you might substitute your inner wisdom or intuition here.

What responses do you get? How do they change or reinforce what you're doing? Our children are a gift and a blessing. Going to the source of wisdom is the best way I know to stay in touch with that fact and act like the guardian of body and soul that we are for our children. I've discovered that he is teaching me to be a mother, if I only listen—not necessarily to what he's asking for, but to what he needs from me and the kind of person he needs me to be. For that, I'm grateful beyond words.

MUST-KNOW INFO

Seven Ways to Stay Connected to the One You Love

Sharon Wegscheider-Cruse, author, Dancing with Destiny *and* Girl Talk: Daily Reflections for Women of All Ages

I f you are married to your sweetheart and you are a mom to a family, you know how hard it is to keep that partnership energy alive and vibrant. There are countless things to do, places to be, and schedules and deadlines to meet. We all have just so many hours in the day. Sometimes we feel overwhelmed and sad as we realize it's been a while since we have felt that "special love." We know the love is there; it just hasn't been felt during busy times.

However, there are ways to keep the passion and connection flamed, and if you try them out, both of you will feel closer to each other. Here are seven possibilities that couples have used and celebrated.

1. **Remember to "reenter."** Because everyone goes in many directions on most work/school days and even on the weekends for a variety of activities, there is a need to "reenter" with each other as a couple at the end of the day. If you plan at

least fifteen minutes or a half hour (if possible) to simply share the day and what you think and how you feel about it, you will feel more connected than if you just keep going your separate ways for the entire day. Reentry has helped couples remember that their relationship is the priority of the day.

2. **Share the load.** Take the time to divide up the family chores in such a way that there is time planned when each person does their home duties. Try to go outside the box in regard to who takes care of the laundry, the cars, the meals, and the shopping. Make some of these duties something you can share with each child, and you will do triple duty. For instance, (a) you get the chores done, (b) each child has some special time with a parent, and (c) you can carve out some time that is just "couple time."

3. **Running the family business.** Statistics show that money woes affect the intimacy of many couples. There are differences of opinion on how money could and should be spent. One or the other partner sometimes hides the amount of money spent on their own wishes, they give each other the silent treatment over an excessive expenditure, or they argue about money wasted or money hoarded. Taking the time to come up with a budget they can both agree on is a way for couples to feel closer to each other. Pick a date of the month and make it a "for sure" time to get together and discuss money. If someone asks either of you to do something that evening, simply tell them that you are booked. You are—with each other. After the meeting, enjoy a treat you both love:

milk shakes, a glass of wine, or a special home movie (with popcorn). Enjoy the closeness that comes from being on top of your financial situation.

4. Share your bedtime. Even though it requires some give and take, try to plan on going to bed together every night you can. It's not about sleeping. It's about knowing you are going to have time together, be able to share the day's happenings, and feel a sense of a special belonging. It's a time to cuddle, to share emotional intimacy, and to let your partner know daily how much you love him or her. Bedtime becomes a ritual that is very special. It is also a powerful lesson for children to learn that parents are a team and need their own time together. It's one way parents can teach their children about relationships.

5. Find some "timeless time." Timeless time is a regularly planned time that has no agenda. We all live with very busy and committed schedules. Cell phones, Blackberries, and Day-Timers all make sure that we meet all of the demands that are on us. Then there are the human demands of children, siblings, in-laws, and friends. To keep energy in a partner relationship, "timeless time" is one way to ensure connection. Choose a half hour a day, a half day a week (a couple of hours at night), or a day on a weekend and just *be* with each other.

Daily you can take a walk (morning or evening), a half day a week or a couple of hours an evening (see a movie, watch a regular TV program), and when possible a day on a weekend (see what is happening in your area). Write the time on the calendar, and then at the last minute decide what it is the two of you want to do together. If you need to arrange babysitting at a regular time each week, then that is the only planning you do. The rest is spontaneous. My husband and I have gone to art fairs, movies, strolled shopping centers, had a special lunch, gone hiking, looked at model homes, visited libraries, and so on. It's always a last-minute surprise. The hard part is scheduling and planning the time. This "timeless time" experience becomes known as your "date time."

6. **Dream together.** Walt Disney said, "If you can dream it, you can do it." Dream together. Dreams start with small conversations and a sharing of something that has yet to happen. You might dream about a different house, a new car, a special vacation, a holiday with family, a holiday away together alone, a change of job, a volunteer job, the loss of ten to fifteen pounds, a regular exercise program, and so on. Dreams are plans waiting to happen. The more dreams you can share, the more you will come to know the thoughts and feelings of your partner. The more you share these dreams, the more possibilities that will happen for both of you.

All of these ways of connecting can nourish your love for each other. The biggest challenge is taking the time. to invest in these behaviors with each other. Sometimes you have to change schedules, priorities, and even friends to make sure you have enough time together. However, if you make the effort, the rewards are huge and very satisfying.

7. **Look at the outside world "as a couple."** Find meaning and purpose outside of your daily happenings and do it as a couple. Maybe you want to join a group of some kind, attend a church or synagogue, volunteer in your community, or go to a workshop together. In recognizing that we are all part of a bigger world, we can find activities that connect us with a larger purpose (something that has meaning for both people). Sometimes my husband and I read the same book and each underline, in a certain color, what stands out for us. Then we read each other's priorities. We know each other better through the author's thoughts and words. We often volunteer for a project together and attend certain functions at a local community center together. It reminds us that we are a small team contributing to a larger world, and we can all make the world a better place to be. In the words of Helen Keller, "Life is either a daring adventure or nothing at all."

MUST-KNOW INFO

Five Ways to Find "Me Time"

Jen Singer, creator, www.mommasaid.net, author
Stop Second-Guessing Yourself—The Toddler Years

For the record, "me time" is not the forty seconds you get between the moment you shut the sliding doors on your minivan and when you open the driver's door. If you're a mom, you know what I'm talking about. You know that "me time" is hard to come by when you're in charge of the kids and the house and whatever that sticky stuff is on the refrigerator door handle.

Chances are, you haven't read beyond your newspaper's headlines in months, maybe years. You recognize only the names of the animated films on the movie marquee, and you only get to put your feet up at the dentist's office. You're starving for "me time," time to recharge, renew, and revitalize.

If you don't take time for yourself now and then, you'll end up tired and cranky, and then what good will you be to your family? The old saying, "If Momma ain't happy, ain't nobody happy," still holds true. Besides, everybody needs a break now and then.

But how can you get "me time" when your life is all about someone (or several someones) else? How can you put the "me" back in Mommy? Here are five tips for finding "me time" when you're the mom:

1. **Remember to schedule your tune-up.** Your car won't run well if you skip its regular tune-ups, and frankly, the same goes for you. Schedule into your calendar regular time off, even if it's just fifteen minutes to hide in a bubble bath at night. But don't stop there. Add a daily walk (sans stroller), a weekly (grown-up) movie out with girl-friends, or a regular date with hubby. And then protect your "me time" from life's little encroachments, like the laundry that's piling up or the kid who needs a ride to his buddy's house right now. Both can wait—or they can be taken care of by someone else. Remember, you've got plans, and, barring an emergency, those plans can't be changed. Your "me time" is your time. Treat it well.

2. **Form your "momtourage."** If you live near other moms with children your kids' ages, it makes it easier to create a "mom-tourage," a group of moms and dads who tag team—parent with you. For example, one mom takes your kids for the morning so you can get some stuff done, and then you take hers the next morning. You carpool to basketball practice with the dad down the street or offer to take the neighbor's kids to the play-ground for an hour or two. Your momtourage will understand when you need to go to the gym or to get a haircut without dragging the kids along, and they'll help you out, just like you help them. Encourage everyone in your momtourage to

schedule in their own "me time," and then plan how to help each other get that time on a regular basis. Soon, every mom (and dad) on the block will be happier, you'll see.

3. Find a hobby that has nothing to do with kids. Face it, scrapbooking is pretty much all about your kids, and so is volunteering for the PTA. While there's no doubt that you can get satisfaction from participating in these sorts of activities, it's good to have something of your own that has nothing to do with motherhood. Maybe you've always wanted to take singing lessons or to train for a marathon. Perhaps you'd like to play soccer again, or maybe you just like to sit in the sauna at the gym for twenty glorious minutes. Whatever your hobby is, if it gets you away from motherhood even for a little while, you'll likely feel more recharged when you return to your family. Find that hobby and then cultivate it so that your "me time" really is all about you.

4. Never say you're "just a mom." When you devalue what you do, you make your time less valuable, too. And why would anyone believe that you need some time to yourself when you've just told them you don't think that motherhood is a worthy role? You don't have to complain about how frazzled you feel either, but you should certainly give yourself the credit you deserve. If you're home with the kids full- or part-time, remind yourself that catering to little kids is indeed a job worthy of time off, just like paid jobs. Everyone needs a break, and you certainly deserve one.

5. **Be a little bit more useless.** The more you jump up to help everyone in the house, the more they'll come to rely on you for every little thing. And that will certainly cut into your "me time." Let your husband search for the butter in the fridge. It's in there, and he'll find it, even without your guidance. Let your kids try a little harder to get their shoes on and their coats zippered. Even the baby can reach her pacifier if you let her try a little harder. Pretend to be too busy to help more often—act a little useless—and soon your family will learn to be more self-sufficient. And then you can get back to that bubble bath you scheduled for tonight.

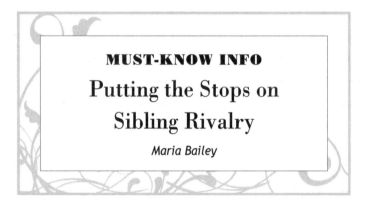

MUST-KNOW INFO

Putting the Stops on Sibling Rivalry

Maria Bailey

T he night I was in labor with my second child, I remember writing a letter to my oldest child apologizing for bringing another baby into our family. As many second-time moms do, I worried about being able to share my love with more than one child. I also worried about establishing the right relationship between siblings. I had heard horror stories about sibling rivalry and the fear that this would somehow enter my family scared me. What I soon learned, however, was that the gift of a brother or sister can be the greatest gift you give your child. The relationship that two siblings share with each other is like no other and resides on a level apart from the parent-child relationship. Setting the foundation for sibling bonding rather than sibling rivalry begins long before the baby arrives and continues well into young adulthood. Here are a few tips toward avoiding sibling rivalry.

1. Involve the big sister or big brother in your pregnancy and preparation for the birth of your baby. Explain the stages of pregnancy and celebrate the milestones in development of both your

children along the way. For instance, in month six, when the baby begins to move, share it with your child but at the same time, mark the month by also focusing on a recent achievement he/she has obtained. The baby is moving in the same month that big brother learned to ride his bike.

2. Ask family and friends to recognize existing children when it's time for shower and homecoming gifts. This small gesture will go a long way to avoiding hurt and resentful feelings in older siblings.

3. Once the new baby is home, allow older siblings to help in the caring for their little brother or sister. Even toddlers can stack diapers or gently push the baby swing.

4. Carve out individual time for each child in the family. This can be as simple as a special bedtime routine with mom to an hour alone in the park with dad. Remember it goes a long way with all age children to look them in the eye when speaking or listening to them. It makes them feel truly connected with you. Take time during baby's nap time to connect with older siblings rather than catching up on housework.

5. Never compare your children with each other. Nothing creates ill feelings between siblings like resentment or jealousy. Refrain from using expressions like, "Why can't you be more like your sister?" or "You are my favorite son." Instead, celebrate the uniqueness of each of your children. If one child is a good artist ask him to share his talents with the family by designing your holiday card or if another is a good cook request that she makes dessert one night.

6. Create projects around your home that allow siblings to work together toward a common goal. You may ask your teenagers to rearrange the basement or entertainment room or allow them to jointly cook dinner for mom and dad one night. It's never too early to develop a strong support system between siblings. At an early age, you can develop games of competition between parents and children such as who can sort the laundry into colors and whites the quickest, table-setting relays, or raking races. The more brothers and sisters learn to work together the less they will want to compete against each other.

7. Never take sides in sibling conflicts. No matter how strong the bond between siblings, a fight is likely to break out at some point. It's actually healthy and allows your child to learn conflict resolution. It's important however to allow your children to work out their differences between themselves. It's okay to give some suggestions for compromise if you feel the need to influence the outcome; however you should never takes sides and pit one child against the other.

8. Lead by example. Talk about your own relationships with your siblings through stories, pictures, and videos. Speak to the love you have for your sisters or brothers and the ways in which they have touched your life. If your relationships with your adult siblings are estranged recount happier childhood experiences or point out pop culture siblings that mirror the relationship you would like your own children to possess.

Brothers and sisters can be an extension of your love for your child that will impact their life long after you are gone. A sibling gives you another human being to share your childhood with and later recount all the moments of growing up in your unique family. It's a person with whom they will share smiles, laughter, tears, and fears and hopefully the desire to create their own sibling relationships with generations to come. With a little bit of effort, you can set the foundation for your child.

Maybe you have a "Tristan." He's the three-year-old who climbs onto the conveyer belt at the Costco checkout and grabs the plastic separator stick to sword-fight with the cashier. In thirteen years of working with families as a psychotherapist and three as a civilian—a mother of what I've come to call my "spirited" child—I've only met a few. So when I meet the parents of a child who seems to be impersonating a young Jerry Lewis, it's a relief to know I'm not alone and it's not my fault that he can be more wild animal than human much of the time.

There are other types of challenging children, such as those who are so sensitive that they notice every tiny change in routine and every tag in their clothing. And there are those who won't eat their cereal if they can't pour the milk themselves, even if much of it ends up on the table instead of in the bowl. In her book *Raising the Spirited Child*, Mary Sheedy Kurcinka says, "The word that distinguishes spirited children from other children is *more.* . . . Spirited kids are the Super Balls in a room full of rubber balls."

A few things we parents of challenging or spirited children

have in common are: (1) We wonder if it's our fault that our child is struggling with issues other children don't; (2) Parents of less-challenging children give us advice as if we've never heard of a time-out; and (3) Our lives are often more intense as we ride along on our child's roller coaster car. Here are some tips you may find helpful on your ride:

1. **Discover what your child really needs from you— and give it to him.** This may include:

- All of your attention. Does your child grab your cell phone and threaten to flush it down the toilet when you're checking your e-mail? He really may need that much attention, especially if he's less than four years old.
- Clear boundaries. "You can only ride your bike to the first driveway, or else your bike gets a time-out."
- Activity. Many spirited children need to be physically tired out twice a day.
- Places to go, people to see. Tristan climbs the walls if he doesn't have a certain amount of novelty in his environment and people to interact with (other than me, of course). So we spend a lot of time with his friends and at local parks.

2. **Conserve your energy.** Unless you're one of those annoying people who wakes up ready for anything on four hours of sleep and without a trip to Starbucks, you'll need to be judicious about how you spend your energy.

Reassess what a clean-enough house looks like; that putting out some goldfish, chicken nuggets, and juice boxes is kind of a dinner party; and that showers don't necessarily happen every day. The good news is that you'll get back your clean house, dinner parties, daily showers, and so much more in a few years.

3. **Get psyched up for the new normal.** Did you just start a riveting conversation with a great mom you've been meaning to get to know, but your child needs to leave the playdate now? Or maybe when you were growing up, your family hosted an annual Thanksgiving feast that would make Martha Stewart envious—and now they are looking to you to continue the tradition.

How do you handle these and other tricky situations? Here are a few ways I've learned to make the right call even when encountering these challenges for the first time or in a public place:

- I remind myself before I arrive at an event that I'll probably have to either shadow my child to keep him from getting too wild, leave an event early even if I want to stay, and/or change my expectations of how we'll spend our time depending on what my son is able to do and what gets his attention. I took him to his first hockey game recently. My goal was for him to have a positive experience. I would have loved to sit in my seat, rooting for my team and leaving at the end of the game. Tristan did not get that memo, and although he sat in his seat for the dramatic introductions, he started losing his ability to focus during the Star-Spangled Banner and was drawing the attention of the usher about the time the puck was dropped because he was climbing the railing next to his seat. Someday we'll sit in our seats and cheer on our team together, but he had a great time and can't wait to go back. According to my new criteria, that was a huge success.

- Use the best part of your day to get things done. Kate, a mother of a spirited four-year-old girl, is a morning person: "If I plan around when I feel energetic, I'm up for anything. But if I make the mistake of thinking that I can have a busy day and then take Anna out for dinner, we almost always end up leaving the restaurant with Anna in tears and me snapping at her to 'grow up.'"

4. Let her know what you want her to do, then catch her being good. It's natural to fall into the trap of reprimanding troublesome behavior. Our days with our spirited children often don't go smoothly. But one secret weapon we have in our arsenal is to let them know what we want them to do and praise them when they do it.

Pam, a mom with a spirited four-year-old who was diagnosed with a mild developmental issue, compares Hunter's behavior to Winnie the Pooh characters. "You feel like Tigger right now, all jumpy and excited. Can you move your body slowly like Eeyore?"

5. Love the one you're with. This is the secret that has helped me the most. I was often at my wit's end with my son, especially before he turned eighteen months old. It seemed that he was either bored and whining or discovering something I didn't want him to get into. But once I started to see the upside of some of his traits and behavior, it was a huge relief.

First, I started telling him that he has so much energy that he's going to be a great daddy someday. Then I realized that I love his curiosity and willingness to try new things. And I really did start loving these traits, even though they wore me out. Eventually, I could picture him at twenty-five years old, entertaining close friends with humorous stories, or being a firefighter or army ranger, using his daring and ingenuity to help others.

Being Tristan's mother is far from my pre-mom mental pictures. But like the other blessings in my life, it's so much richer and more amazing that I could have imagined.

MUST-KNOW INFO

When Playdates Replace Grown-Up Dates: Tips on Great Sex

Heidi Raykeil, author of Confessions of a Naughty Mommy: How I Found My Lost Libido *and* Love in the Time of Colic: The New Parent's Guide to Getting It on Again

I'm sure you can relate: Your smooth-jazz CDs have been replaced by the Wiggles; your plush satin bed pillows have been replaced by a board book of *Goodnight, Moon*, and date night now involves a trip to Home Depot to buy mulch. It's no wonder many women feel sapped or uninspired in the bedroom. Yet having a healthy sex life is as much for you as it is for hubby. Here are some tips to getting things going in the bedroom department.

1. **Forget Trying to Be Hot Mama and Go for Hot Moments Instead.** With the surge of Hollywood moms out there it's easier than ever to feel frumpy and fat in your own (sometimes all too real) life. Unfortunately, hotness has become another expectation for new mothers, right up there with seamlessly juggling career and family and generally running the world. Well, real moms don't have private chefs and personal trainers. We have potty training! And while shaving our legs and getting a

makeover might indeed help some of us feel sexier, truly redis-covering our sexual selves takes a lot more inner work and a lot more outer acceptance. Our sexiness begins and ends with us. It's not up to others to tell us we're sexy, whether it's society or our husbands. So stop shooting for mythical hot mom status, and start trying to rediscover hot moments instead. When you find your-self having a sexual or sensual thought, no matter how small, try to follow it and get to the root. You don't have to do anything about it, just explore how it feels. Explore yourself, too. Your body is different now, it's time to get to know it again. And remem-ber—no matter how far gone your libido may seem at times, there is still a sexual person under there. Just a really tired one.

2. **Get Turned Off to Get Turned On.** New research shows that for a woman to get turned on, other parts of her brain actually need to be turned off. Finally, proof that walking by a stack of dirty dishes really does turn a woman off! Similarly, many first time dads report sexual problems they never expe-rienced before. For some it's the stress of providing for their new family, for others it's a result of feeling left out or seeing their wife in a new light as mother. So how do you turn off the worry, anxiety, and just plain old overwhelming mother-love so you can get some other love going again? We each need to do our parts; dads need to step up with baby care and housework and mom needs to back off and let them. And both need to work to see each other not only as parents but as the lovers and friends that got this whole thing going. Start by commit-ting to date night once a week. It's a chance to share and

reconnect, to see the big picture stuff and clear your heads of the day to day minutaie of child-rearing. If you can't or don't want to leave the baby with a sitter, be creative: schedule date day at naptime, plan a date for after the baby goes to bed, or just take turns reading to each other in the bath. (No parenting books!) The more you practice turning off mom and dad brains, the more you'll find you're turning on other, more fun, parts of each other.

3. **Focus on Quality, Not Quantity.** Don't judge your new sex life against your friends' (don't believe them!) or your pre-baby one. It's a zero sum game. But that doesn't mean the game is over. In fact, many couples find their sex lives have become much richer after having kids. Now is the time to make the sex you do have really count. Think of this as a time to turn over a new sexual leaf. It's time to build the sex life you really want and deserve. Open a real dialog about sex and what it means to you as a couple, what you like and don't like. Be as specific as you can. This is no time to be shy, because, frankly, who has time for much of anything now anyway? Commit to truly being present in your body and with each other when you make love. Let yourself go into the moment, and open up fully to each other and the experience. Yes, you might be having sex less, but you don't have to feel sexless.

4. **That Said, Quantity Does Matter. . . .** Sometimes, like the commercial says, you just have to do it. With these new busy lives it's too easy to forget that sex is something that matters. It's too easy to slip into our parent roles and slip away from true

connection. But now is when we need that connection most. So jump on in and give it a try. Remember that making love is a form of communication. What you can say in those few quick minutes (it really doesn't take that long, folks . . .) can make a world of difference in your relationship. If you find you can't let go and relax, or if you're having physical or mental problems that continue to interfere with your sex life, talk to your doctor or a therapist and get the help you need to have a fun and satisfying sex life through parenthood and beyond.

Combining family and work under one roof does have its challenges. But with a little juggling, a lot of humor, and these tried-and-true survival strategies, it's possible to be successful at both. In fact, Ellen Parlapiano and Patricia Cobe have over twenty-five years experience juggling motherhood and home businesses. They coined and trademarked the term "Mompreneurs" in the 1990s. Here are their tips for work-at-home moms.

Tap into your parenting skills. Running a business is a lot like raising children. You have to be well organized, disciplined, nurturing, adept at multitasking, good at relationship building, and able to shift gears quickly. These are skills that mothers use everyday—which is why moms make such great entrepreneurs.

Go in with a plan. Like a road map, a business plan helps you chart your course. Every business should include a mission statement, business goals, a marketing plan, and estimates of start-up costs and earning expectations. Figure in child care, too—

especially for babies and preschoolers. While it's possible to work around naps and into the wee hours of the night, part-time child care can prevent burnout. It doesn't have to cost a bundle—many work-at-home moms swap babysitting, hire teenagers, and find other affordable solutions.

Set office hours. It's important to protect your work and family time with a clearly defined schedule. When you run your own business, working nights and weekends can become a fact of life. But you'll be a lot more productive—and a lot less stressed—if you set a schedule for yourself. Decide when you'll work, and when you won't. *Never* take your laptop to bed. And close your office door at the end of your workday—even if you don't have a real door!

Roll with the punches. Expect your best-laid plans to go berserk when a child gets sick or you have a plumber in your house all day fixing broken pipes. Flexibility is an essential job requirement for mompreneurs. So don't beat yourself up if you lose a few precious hours of work time. Instead, drop your 9 to 5 mind-set and learn to work in spurts, getting back on track as soon as you can.

Build a strong support system. Spouses, parents, friends, neighbors, and colleagues can be your safety net when that fragile work/family balance tips (see "sick child" and "plumbing emergency" above!). Make sure those closest to you realize that you are serious about your business so they will readily come to your rescue in times of need. Involve your children from an early age so they understand what you do and respect your work time. It's okay to show off a little, too. Volunteer to talk about your business in your children's classes or at a career fair. You'll be enhancing your own professional image and that of all work-from-home moms.

Network, network, network. When you work in solitude, it's crucial to connect with colleagues, clients, and customers—both face-to-face and virtually. Social networks like Facebook, LinkedIn, and Twitter are an invaluable resource for generating buzz about your biz. Online communities and blogs are key in helping you forge bonds with like-minded businesswomen and providing a place to share tips and test ideas. But be selective; be careful not to fritter away precious work time by constantly chatting in online forums. And don't forget—home-based doesn't mean housebound. Get involved in professional organizations and women's business groups, and attend the meetings. Better yet, volunteer to be on the board of one group that is especially relevant to your business. You'll find that other women entrepreneurs are usually more than happy to share their strategies and lessons learned.

Be your own spin doctor. Talk up your business wherever you go—whether it's at a Chamber of Commerce luncheon, PTA meeting, or the sidelines of your child's soccer game. Always have business cards on hand. And develop a website that's a showcase for you and your enterprise. It should be easy to navigate, featuring your logo, testimonials from satisfied customers, press releases, and other company news. Update your website regularly to keep it cutting-edge, and drive traffic to your site with strategic search engine optimization (SEO). Many mom entrepreneurs are forging alliances to strengthen their marketing muscle. Cooperative marketing—small businesses banding together to promote and publicize themselves—increases your clout without increasing your expenditures.

Cultivate confidence. When you work in isolation, you often have to be your own cheering squad. Always remind yourself of your successes, especially on those impossible days when nothing seems to be going right. An "I can do it" attitude will take you far; confidence is contagious—when you have it, you'll pass it along to everyone around you.

Grow at your own pace. Mom-owned businesses tend to grow organically, nurtured along much like mothers nurture their children. Enterprises that grow slowly and steadily allow for more control over work/family time and more flexibility. They are less risky, too—no venture capitalists or hungry investors looking to pull the plug if profits aren't substantial enough. While it's important to keep the payroll small while you're in growth mode, it's also essential to delegate when necessary. It all comes back to achieving the balance that all moms crave—the balance between their professional and personal lives so neither has to be sacrificed for the other.

Laugh often. When kids and work occupy the same space, hilarious things can happen. Although it might be embarrassing to have your two-year-old yell "I have to go potty" when you're on the phone with a prospective client, you have to have a sense of humor. A little laughter goes a long way in diffusing potentially stressful situations. And most times, that client on the other end of the phone will laugh with you.

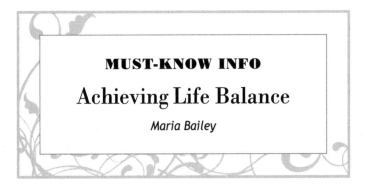

MUST-KNOW INFO

Achieving Life Balance

Maria Bailey

As moms, it seems to be our very nature to make sure that everyone else's needs are met before our own. The tugging and pulling at our time and emotions as well as the physical inabilities to do so much can easily create a state of imbalance. Although there are simple ways to gain a sense of balance in your life, it is important to remember that "balance" is a state of being that is constantly changing and requires constant alterations to maintain. It's always important to remember that it's okay to have imbalance sometimes. In fact, when you recognize that you are feeling a bit out of balance, you gain a sense of relief knowing you are in control of the emotion and change is just around the corner.

From one busy mom to another, here are some ways to find family/work and self balance:

Define Your Values and Priorities. The feeling of imbalance occurs when we are *doing* things that do not align with the priorities we feel. In other words our actions do not reflect our inner emotions. For example, as a mom you might value time with your children but as a homemaker, cleaning the garage becomes a priority. As a result you become frustrated because you are spending all day cleaning the garage instead of playing with your children. To find more balance in your life, make a list of your values and beside it write a list of your priorities as you see them today. Now draw a line between items on the two lists that are aligned. Those priorities that do not support your values are the tasks in your day throwing you into that sense of imbalance. To find balance, alter your lists to create a steady scale.

Do a Time Audit. When a person is in financial trouble, professionals advise conducting a financial audit of spending to see where changes can be made. Time is the currency of most moms trying to seek work/life balance so when life is out of balance it's time for a Time Audit. It's easy to do and a great way to recapture lost time in your day. For three days (one weekend and two weekdays) write down everything you do and the time associated with it. For instance, you may find you spend ten minutes searching for your child's lost homework and school papers every morning. Write it down. At the end of the three days, look over your days and ask these questions. Can I live without doing this every day? How can I reorganize or change the situation that allows me to loose time on this task? Who can help me do this task to save me time? By taking a long detailed look at the way you spend your money or in this case, your time, you are certain to find a few minutes to spend more efficiently or selfishly.

Keep stomachs full and happy. Sixty-five percent of mothers, according to BSM Media research, do not know what they are cooking for dinner at 4 PM. Meal planning and feeding our family is one of the most stressful activities we do, particularly since hunger only intensifies cranky moods caused by fatigue. With a little bit of planning, mothers can turn the bewitching hours around dinner into a time that is more enjoyable and stress free. First, plan ahead. This might be as simple as knowing what you are cooking for the next two nights or as detailed as a week's worth of menus. I cook most of my meals on Sunday utilizing a simple category system. Monday night is always crock-pot night. This allows me to throw a meat, vegetables, and potatoes into the pot on Sunday night and just plug it in on Monday morning. I roast a chicken or turkey and during the week it is sliced, diced on a salad, or stirred into a casserole. Pasta sauce is easily stored and it only takes minutes to boil noodles as a quick homemade fix.

Create a Family Communication Center. Balancing schedules is one of the greatest challenges for moms. Between sports, homework, book club, and possibly work, moms have a lot going on in their daily routines. No one likes surprises when trying to keep it all straight. Create a family communication center by hanging a large bulletin board in a common area of your home. Attach a large calendar and assign a different color marker for each member of the family. Instruct everyone to write their commitments and schedules on the family calendar. For papers that need mom attention, hang an "in" box and "out" box next to the communication center. Instruct kids to leave papers that need your attention in the "in" box and allow them to pick up completed sheets in your "out" box. This will eliminate chaotic mornings of lost permission slips or school papers.

Exercise. Who would imagine that the law of physics would work in balancing life as moms? Remember "For every action or reaction there is an equal action or reaction?" or "An object in motion stays in motion?" These rules ring true in creating the momentum for your family. If mom is tired and dragging, family life is likely to imitate the energy level. Make exercise a priority each and every day. You don't have to run a marathon; just move your body. The energy you expend devoting yourself to self-wellness will not only give you more energy but set a good example to your family that health and fitness is important. Exercise can also be a great way to meditate on your day, create much needed alone time, or be done with children as a family activity.

Implementing only a few of these strategies will help busy moms find the twenty-fifth hour in their day or gain a sense of balance along the way.

The Writers

Judy L. Adourian is a freelance writer and writing coach. She has been published in *Because It Works*, four editions of the *A Cup of Comfort* series, *Grab Your Tiger*, *Underwired*, *Apollo's Lyre*, *LitWit*, and the *Providence Journal*.

Missing adventure genes, **B. J. Bateman** has sought recognition in writing. She has had two short stories and three essays published and has won a first place award in both fiction and nonfiction and placed third in a short story competition. She continues to nurture her ink genes.

Jane Koenen Bretl is a freelance writer and photographer who resides in West Chester, Ohio, with her understanding husband and two fine sons. After a decade in the food industry, she (truly) sees her career as a mom as her most fulfilling position. If not gardening, she might be found blogging at http://janebretl.wordpress.com.

Sandy Foster Brooks is a freelance writer who lives in Lee's Summit, Missouri, with her husband, two children, one dog, two cats, and a frog. She enjoys reading, cooking, gardening, and being a Kool-Aid Mom herself.

Marcia E. Brown, who lives in Austin, Texas, became a full-time freelance writer when family stories she wrote for her son began to sell to national publications. She has been published in magazines, newspapers, and a dozen anthologies. Several of her stories have won awards. She is a member of the National League of American Pen Women and Writers League of Texas.

Minnie N. Browne is married to Dr. J. Browne. They have two children and four grandchildren. She's a writer, artist, retired school teacher, a court-appointed child advocate, active in her church, been published in the Chicken Soup Series, the magazine *Granbury Showcase*, and the *Langdon Review of the Arts in Texas*.

Kathe Campbell lives on a Montana mountain with her mammoth donkeys, a keeshond, and a few kitties. She is a prolific writer on Alzheimer's, and her stories can be found on many e-zines. Kathe is a contributing author to the Chicken Soup for the Soul series, numerous anthologies, RX for Writers website, and medical journals. E-mail her at kathe@wildblue.net.

Emily Parke Chase is the author of *Help! My Family's Messed Up!* (Kregel, 2008) and speaks hundreds of times each year about family relationships. Her three children are now grown up and are starting families of their own, but the family still welcomes all the love that comes from her new stepmother. Learn more about Emily at emily-chase.com.

Helen Colella is a freelance writer from Colorado. Her work includes educational materials, articles/stories for adults and children, contributions to Chicken Soup for the Soul books and parenting magazines across the country. She also operates AssistWrite, assistwrite@comcast.net, a home-based-business offering writing services to independent publishers.

Cookie Curci was born and raised in San Jose, California, where she lives with her family and little dog, Zuzu. She has a bounty of stories and memories inspired by her creative mom and her close-knit family. Cookie has recorded these memories for the next generation to learn from and to enjoy.

Gabrielle F. Descoteaux, born in Montreal, Quebec, Canada in 1915, graduated St. Gregory School in Detroit, Michigan, then worked in various retail stores. She married Joe Lesjack in St. Benedict Church, Highland Park, Michigan, and moved to Warren Township. Gabrielle and Joe's fifth and sixth children arrived during the construction of the family home. Gabrielle, who threw right but batted left, became a widow in 1948. She used her husband's life insurance money to pay off the house and raised six children by herself in the ancestral home. Her oldest daughter died in 1995. Gabrielle died in 2002 in the presence of the two daughters featured in "The Chase." She was eighty-seven years of age.

Terri Elders previously wrote about her mother and Halloween in "Tea for Two" in *Chicken Soup for the Soul: A Tribute to Moms*. Though a lifetime writer and editor, she just recently began memorializing family, friends, and pets through anthology contributions. Write her at telders@hotmail.com.

Jean M. Fogle is the author of *Salty Dogs*, a photography book of dogs enjoying the beach, published by Wiley. She writes about gardening and dog topics and her work has appeared in many national publications and books. You can visit her website at http://jeanmfogle.com and her blog Pixels-n-Pen—Life in the Freelance Lane at http://pixels-n-pen.blogspot.com. She lives in Fort Valley Virginia.

Peggy Frezon is the winner of *Guideposts* writers contest in 2004, and The Children's Writer personal story contest in 2007. Publishing credits include *Guideposts*, Teaching Tolerance, Positive Thinking, Pockets, Chicken Soup for the Soul and others. She's currently writing a book about dogs and diets. Please visit her blog, "The Writer's Dog" at thewritersdog.blogspot.com

Marilyn A. Gelman has never traveled abroad nor seen much outside of New Jersey. Her publication credits include *The New York Times*, *A Cup of Comfort for Dog Lovers*, *A Cup of Comfort for Divorced Women*, *Creative Nonfiction*, and *True Confessions*. She is an advocate for people living with traumatic brain injury and other "invisible" disabilities.

Louis A. Hill Jr. authored three books and many articles. He earned a Ph.D. in structural engineering, designed bridges and buildings and joined the engineering faculty at Arizona State University. He retired an Emeritus Dean of Engineering from The University of Akron. He is listed in Who's Who in America.

Colleen Ferris Holz is a freelance writer who lives in Appleton, Wisconsin, with her husband and two sons. She is also a volunteer coordinator for a mentoring program for families living in poverty. She is currently researching effective mentoring methods to write a guidebook for volunteers.

Patricia Hoyt received her master's degree in education from the University of Oregon. She taught elementary school for more than twenty years and is now happily retired. Patricia spends her extra time raising chickens, teaching water aerobics, gardening, and working with the youth at her church. She has previously published a story in *Chicken Soup to Inspire a Woman's Soul* and *Chicken Soup for the Coffee Lover's Soul*.

Georgia A. Hubley retired after twenty years in financial management to write full-time. She's a frequent contributor to the Chicken Soup for the Soul series, *Christian Science Monitor*, and numerous other magazines, newspapers, and anthologies. She resides with her husband of thirty years in Henderson, Nevada. Contact her at GEOHUB@aol.com.

Ellen Javernick is a second grade teacher in Loveland, Colorado. She enjoys a second career as a writer. Her most recently published children's book is *The Birthday Pet*. She's Grams to eight adorable grandchildren. E-mail her at javernicke@aol.com.

Mimi Greenwood Knight is a freelance writer living in southern Louisiana with her husband, David, four kids, three dogs, two cats, and a fish called Gilligan. She has more than three hundred published articles and essays in magazines, anthologies, and on websites. Mimi enjoys butterfly gardening, Bible study, and the lost art of letter writing.

Tina Koenig is a publicist, journalist, and short story writer. She mentors emerging writers through guided writing workshops held at the Florida Center for the Book in Fort Lauderdale, Florida.

John J. Lesjack, a retired educator, has been published in several Chicken Soup for the Soul books, the *San Francisco Chronicle Sunday Magazine*, *Grit*, and other publications. His mother, Gabrielle F. Descoteaux, passed away in 2002. She left behind six children, seventeen grandchildren, and two great-grandchildren, and they all miss her and the games she played with them. Jlesjack@gmail.com.

Tracy Line is a freelance writer and an editor with Current Publications. Her work has appeared in a variety of magazines and newspapers. She is married and has three beautiful daughters. For writing or reprint information, please contact her at Tracy.Line@comcast.net.

Andrea Marcusa's essays have been published or are forthcoming in the *Christian Science Monitor*, the *Copper Nickel*, the *New York Times*, and other publications. She was a finalist in the *Ontario Review*'s 2007 fiction competition.

Roberta McGovern is the mother of two and grandmother of four, originally from Chelmsford, Massachusetts, but relocated to Marco Island, Florida, almost thirty years ago. Roberta and her husband of forty-four years now live in "The Villages," a retirement community near Ocala, Florida, where they are enjoying every minute of life. Roberta will soon be retired after forty-five years as a nurse.

Michelle L. Miller, Ph.D., is the author of four books and is an award-winning producer and host of *Public Affairs Health Talk Radio* in Dallas, Texas. Portions of this story were excerpted from her book, *On My Way: A Monumental Cancer Battle Revealed.*

Judi Moreo is a motivational speaker and the author of the award-winning book, *You Are More Than Enough: Every Woman's Guide to Purpose, Passion, and Power.* Her enthusiasm for living an extraordinary life is mirrored in her zeal for helping others realize their potential and achieve their goal. Contact her at judi@judimoreo.com; (702) 896-2228.

Amy Mullis lives in upstate South Carolina where, with Mom as a guide, she discovered that the path to the heart is best shared with friends of all kinds. Find more of her work in *The Ultimate Cat Lover*, thewahmmagazine.com (where she writes a humor column), or on her blog at www.mindovermullis.blogspot.com.

Marilyn Nutter has been a contributor to several compilations, including *Chicken Soup for the Mother of Preschooler's Soul* and *Laundry Tales*. She is the author of *Dressed Up Moms' Devotions to Go* and *Tea Lover's Devotions to Go*. Her most recent book is *Diva Delights Devotions to Go* (2009). As a mother, grandmother, and former Mother of Preschoolers (MOPS) mentor, Marilyn enjoys speaking to MOPS and women's groups about finding extraordinary treasures in ordinary days. Visit her website at www.marilynnutter.com.

Rachel Wallace-Oberle writes for various magazines, newspapers, anthologies, and agencies, some of which have taken her from the broadcasting booth to the mountains of rural Haiti. She is one of the founding members of Faith FM 94.3, the first Christian radio station in Kitchener, Ontario. Her work has appeared in publications such as *Reader's Digest, Homemakers, Canadian Living, Woman's World, Today's Parent*, Chicken Soup for the Soul and Cup of Comfort books.

Linda O'Connell's essays, poetry, prose, and articles have been published in numerous periodicals, anthologies, literary magazines, and newspapers. She and her husband, Bill, enjoy gardening and spending time with their nine grandchildren. Linda is happiest when walking on a beach. She has been an early childhood educator in St. Louis, Missouri, for three decades. You can contact her at billin7@juno.com.

Todd Outcalt is the author of seventeen books, including the HCI titles *The Best Things in Life Are Free* and *The Healing Touch*. He lives in Brownsburg, Indiana, with his wife and two children.

Ava Pennington is a freelance writer and speaker with an MBA from St. John's University and a Bible studies certificate from Moody Bible Institute. She has published magazine articles and contributed stories to ten Chicken Soup for the Soul books and two Cup of Comfort books. Learn more at www.avawrites.com.

Linda Kaullen Perkins's short stories, articles, and essays have appeared in various publications, including *Chicken Soup for the Chocolate Lover's Soul, Chicken Soup for the Soul Kids in the Kitchen, Country Woman* magazine and *Woman's World* magazine. Visit Linda at www.lindakperkins.com.

Connie K. Pombo is an author, speaker, and founder of Women's Mentoring Ministries in Mount Joy, Pennsylvania. When not speaking or writing, Connie enjoys photography —one of her greatest passions. You can reach her at www.conniepombo.com.

Sallie A. Rodman is an award-winning author with stories in numerous anthologies (including the Chicken Soup and Cup of Comfort series), magazines, and the *Orange County Register* newspaper. She resides in Los Alamitos, California, with her husband, Paul, and Inky the cat. Reach her at sa.rodman@verizon.net.

Wayne Scheer retired from college teaching to follow his own advice and write. He's been nominated for a Pushcart Prize and a Best of the Net award. His work has appeared in *Notre Dame Magazine*, the *Christian Science Monitor*, and *Pedestal Magazine*, among others. Wayne lives in Atlanta with his wife and can be contacted at wvscheer@aol.com.

Jacqueline Seewald has taught writing courses at the high school, middle school, and college level and has also worked as an academic librarian and educational media specialist. Seven of her novels have been published and her short stories, poems, essays, reviews, and articles have appeared in numerous publications, including the *Christian Science Monitor, After Dark, Library Journal, and Publisher's Weekly*, among others. Her romantic suspense/mystery thriller, *The Inferno Collection* (Five Star/Gale) was published in 2007 and a large-print edition was published by Wheeler in 2008. A sequel, *The Drowning Pool*, is scheduled for publication in February 2009.

Michael Jordan Segal married his high school sweetheart, Sharon, and became a father to their daughter, Shawn. Mike is a social worker at Memorial Hermann Hospital in Houston, Texas, and is currently working on two book projects: an autobiography, and an anthology of his short stories. Mike's CD of twelve of his inspiring stories, entitled *Possible*, is available on his website. He is also a popular inspirational speaker, sharing his recipe for success, happiness, and recovery. Please visit his website, www.InspirationByMike.com, or call Sterling International Speakers Bureau, toll-free in the USA/Canada, at 1-877-226-1003 for more information.

Ryma Shohami is a technical writer/editor. She lives in Israel with her husband and two daughters. Visit her blog Write It Down! at http://rymashohami.wordpress.com. A website devoted to muffins is still under construction. Ryma dreams of spending a year in her log house in Prince Edward Island and of someday swimming with dolphins in Hawaii.

Joyce Stark lives in Northeast Scotland and recently retired from local government. She has written a travel guide to the United States, based on her travels throughout the States. She has also written a children's series aiming to teach a second language to very young children. Contact her at joric.stark@virgin.net.

Jill Sunshine grew up in San Diego, California, where her parents introduced her to the wonders of the world through reading and camping trips. She, like her imaginative mother, is a public school teacher. She lives with her husband, Aparajit, who encourages her to write. She may be reached at jillsunshine.writer@gmail.com.

Annmarie B. Tait resides in Conshohocken, Pennsylvania, with her husband, Joe, and Sammy the Wonder Yorkie. In addition to writing stories about her large Irish Catholic family and the memories they made, Annmarie also enjoys singing and recording Irish and American folk songs. Contact Annmarie at irishbloom@aol.com.

Cynthia Thrift, a freelance writer from the southeast, is married to a very sexy chef, is a tireless primary caregiver to her three children (who are four, three, and two), and writes, huddled in a makeshift office, after the children go to bed. She is the wearer of many hats, including—but never limited to—laundry lady, chef, banker, accountant, schedule coordinator, referee, playmate, lover, friend, daughter, and sister.

Nancy Viau is a freelance writer from New Jersey, and author of a novel for children ages eight to twelve titled *Samantha Hansen Has Rocks in Her Head* (Abrams/Amulet, 2008). Visit her on the Web at www.nancyviau.com.

Judy Wilson's life as a wife and mom has seen significant changes this year. Elissa married two days after graduating from the military academy, Judy's youngest child graduated from high school and went to college, and in between these events, she left her home of thirty years and moved to New Hampshire. She is grateful beyond words for God's presence through it all and that her husband and best friend Tony was by her side.

Ferida Wolff is the author of seventeen books for children including *The Story Blanket* and *Is a Worry Worrying You?* both picture books written with Harriet May Savitz. Her essays appear in anthologies, newspapers, and magazines as well as online. Visit her at her website www.feridawolff.com.

D. B. Zane is a writer and teacher. She has been published in Chicken Soup books and elsewhere. When not teaching or spending time with her three children, she coaches and judges middle school debate.

The Must-Know Experts

Sharon Wegscheider-Cruse is a nationally known consultant, educator, speaker, and author. She is also the founder of several family treatment programs including Onsite Workshops in Tennessee. (Onsite has treated and trained over 35,000+ people.) She is a family therapist with a specialty in addictions. She has conducted workshops around the world and has consulted with military, school systems, treatment centers, and corporations. She has appeared on *The Oprah Winfrey Show, Good Morning American, Phil Donahue,* and *Larry King*. She has written seventeen books. Many have been translated into French, German, Spanish, Greek, Portuguese, and Japanese. She is the subject of several DVDs that are used for training purposes. She is known for her development of the Family Roles: Family Hero, Scapegoat, Lost Child, and Mascot. Sharon and her books are available at www.sharonwcruse.com.

Leslie Godwin has been a psychotherapist for over twenty years, and an entrepreneur for the last ten years, creating a type of Career & Life-Transition Coaching that helps people put their families, faith, and principles first when making career and life choices. Leslie works out of her Calabasas office as a Career & Life-Transition Coach and writer. Leslie has been a resource for the *Wall Street Journal*, Businessweek.com, *Fortune*, USAToday.com, CNN, LIFETIME television network, *Ladies Home Journal, Entrepreneur, Los Angeles Times, Los Angeles Daily News*, www.DrLaura.com, and other print and online media.

Ellen H. Parlapiano and **Patricia Cobe** are experts on mom-owned businesses, and authors of the books, *Mompreneurs®: A Mother's Practical Step-by-Step Guide to Work-at-Home Success* and *Mompreneurs® Online: Using the Internet to Build Work@Home Success*. They also run MompreneursOnline.com, a Web community that connects mom business owners. Their Mompreneurs® Marketplace helps mom entrepreneurs market their products and services. Between them, Parlapiano and Cobe have over twenty-five years experience juggling motherhood and home businesses. They own the trademark to the brand Mompreneurs®, and are the only ones in the United States legally allowed to use it in commerce.

Heidi Raykeil, aka the "Naughty Mommy," enjoys a wonderful and mostly tame life with her husband and two daughters in Seattle. She is the author of the book, *Confes-*

sions of a Naughty Mommy: How I Found My Lost Libido (Seal Press, 2006) and *Love in the Time of Colic: The New Parents' Guide to Getting It on Again* (Collins, 2009). Her writing has been featured online at *Literary Mama* and in *Parenting* magazine. She is a contributor to several anthologies and books, including *Our Bodies, Our Selves: Pregnancy and Childbirth* (The Boston Women's Health Collective, 2008), *Literary Mama: Reading for the Maternally Inclined* (2008), and *Unbuttoned* (forthcoming). She has appeared on *Today, The Situation With Tucker Carlson,* and various local and national media.

Jen Singer is the mother of two tween boys who talk to her through the bathroom door. She is the author of a three-book parenting series called, *MommaSaid.net presents: Stop Second Guessing Yourself.* Jen writes the Good Grief: A Tale of Two Tweens blog for Good Housekeeping.com, which is syndicated on Yahoo! Shine. She is the creator of MommaSaid.net, the back fence of the Internet and a Forbes Best of the Web community for moms. She is the creator of *"Please* Take My Children to Work Day," a holiday for stay-at-home moms celebrated on the last Monday each June, which has been officially proclaimed by governors in a dozen states so far. A cancer survivor, Jen is the Parenting with Cancer moderator at Planet Cancer and aspires to be the loudest voice for the Leukemia and Lymphoma Society.

About the Author

Known as the voice of moms, **Maria Bailey** is an award-winning author, radio talk show host, international speaker, and the foremost authority on marketing to moms. Every day she speaks to approximately 8 million mothers online, on-air, and in print. She is host of *Mom Talk Radio* (www.momtalkradio.com) and cohost of *Good Day with Doug Stephan*, the number seven morning drive-time radio show. She is the founder of BlueSuitMom.com (www.bluesuitmom.com), an award-winning website for working mothers and cofounder of Newbaby.com (www.newbaby.com), a video portal for mothers. Maria is a featured writer in many parenting publications, including *OC Family Magazine*. Professionally, Maria is CEO of BSM Media (www.bsmmedia.com), a full-service marketing and media firm that specializes in connecting companies with mothers. Her clients include Disney, Precious Moments, Hewlett-Packard, and Avon. She is the author of *Marketing to Moms: Getting Your Share of the Trillion Dollar Market, Trillion Dollar Moms: Marketing to a New Generation of Mothers*, and *Mom 3.0: Marketing with Today's Mothers by Leveraging New Media and Technology*. Maria blogs at www.bluesuitmom.com/blog and www.myteenthealien.com. You can follow her on Facebook and Twitter at Mom Talk Radio.

Copyright Credits

(continued from page ii)